Akashic Records and Twin Flames

An Essential Guide to the Secret Nature of the Akasha and Attracting Your Twin Flame

© Copyright 2021

All Rights Reserved. No part of this book may be reproduced in any form without permission in writing from the author. Reviewers may quote brief passages in reviews.

Disclaimer: No part of this publication may be reproduced or transmitted in any form or by any means, mechanical or electronic, including photocopying or recording, or by any information storage and retrieval system, or transmitted by email without permission in writing from the publisher.

While all attempts have been made to verify the information provided in this publication, neither the author nor the publisher assumes any responsibility for errors, omissions or contrary interpretations of the subject matter herein.

This book is for entertainment purposes only. The views expressed are those of the author alone, and should not be taken as expert instruction or commands. The reader is responsible for his or her own actions.

Adherence to all applicable laws and regulations, including international, federal, state and local laws governing professional licensing, business practices, advertising and all other aspects of doing business in the US, Canada, UK or any other jurisdiction is the sole responsibility of the purchaser or reader.

Neither the author nor the publisher assumes any responsibility or liability whatsoever on the behalf of the purchaser or reader of these materials. Any perceived slight of any individual or organization is purely unintentional.

Your Free Gift (only available for a limited time)

Thanks for getting this book! If you want to learn more about various spirituality topics, then join Mari Silva's community and get a free guided meditation MP3 for awakening your third eye. This guided meditation mp3 is designed to open and strengthen ones third eye so you can experience a higher state of consciousness. Simply visit the link below the image to get started.

https://spiritualityspot.com/meditation

Contents

Part 1: Akashic Records

Unlocking the Secret Universal Knowledge and Nature of the Akasha Including Prayer, Guided Meditation, and Akashic Tarot Reading

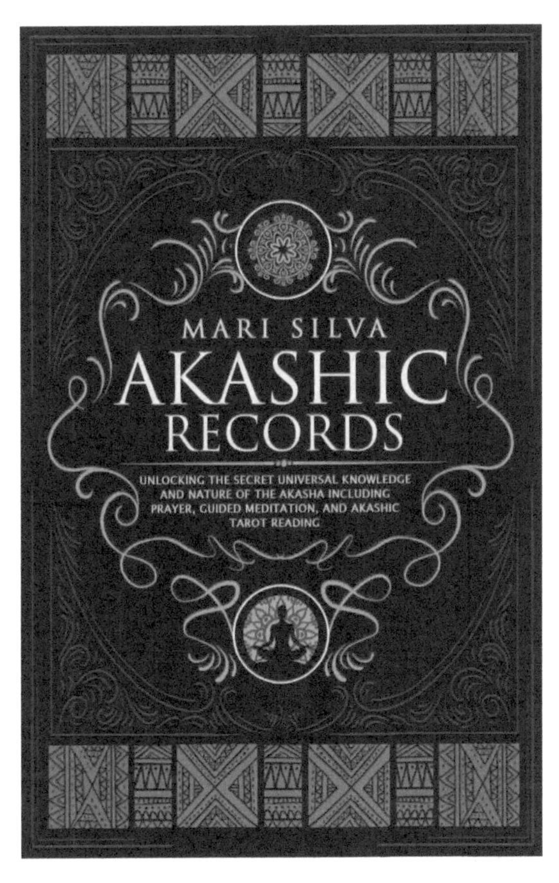

Introduction

Opening the Akashic Records of one's self is a tremendous feat. Gaining access to the invisible yet powerful vibrations that control the flow of the universe may sound like science-fiction, but it is not. Before you begin on your journey, I highly advise you to stop and take a few deep breaths. The journey you're about to embark on will change the course of your destiny, and the destiny of those around you. Every time you begin or end your reading session, accompany it with a few preparative deep and conscious breaths. This will set your intentions straight because you'll be able to dedicate your full attention to what you read.

Preparing your heart is as important as preparing your mind when accepting the information, you'll read, along with practicing the exercises. While the roots of Akashic Records are buried deep in ancient practices, there is a lot of recently discovered information in this book that will help you gain access to your records smoothly. You'll gain new knowledge about stuck emotions that are vibrating at bad frequencies, and you'll gain knowledge about transforming them into higher and more joyous vibrations. You'll begin by finding lingering wounds in your past, not just in this life, but past lives too.

The healing process is difficult, but once people find their way through Akashic Records, it becomes much easier than people think. Introduction to karma and karmic patterns will help you gain enough insight into the historical roots that could be binding you in plateaus of low vibrations. While the information presented here won't instill the power of change within you, it will make sure that it maximizes and amplifies the efforts you make to transform yourself. Joy is one of the main motivations for people to access the Akashic Records, and for a good reason.

You've probably tried to attract joy, and the results have been mostly underwhelming. And that's normal, at first. Once you awaken the true power of joy within you through the Akashic Records, you'll be able to see how vibrations and energy can easily influence you and your environment. The more time you spend in the Akashic Records, the more you'll be able to properly sense joy. Attracting joy will be no problem because you'll understand the very basic dynamics that control it, through your direct access to the Akashic Records.

Using the energies and vibrations flowing through your Akashic Records will give you the potential to manifest your deepest and most genuine desires. This manifestation is the product of seeing the world from a non-linear perspective, which opens up a world of opportunities blocked by a web of illusions. The limitations imposed upon you are, sadly, all internalized, designed to stop you from seeing the full truth. It is your responsibility to remove these restrictions through the Akashic Records.

Growth isn't the end goal. You're bound to grow with or without the Akashic Records. Stopping the flow of time and energy is impossible, but unique individuals can add to and improve upon the collective vibrations that bind us. The challenges you will encounter will not be easy, but each entanglement you unwind through the Akashic Records will be your ally.

Not everyone can comfortably talk about why they love themselves. Sadly, most of the time, people don't love themselves as much as they need to. No external force can make you love yourself, whether you're in a relationship with a loving person or if it's your family that loves you. Bearing the load of karmic patterns and past traumatic events makes it very hard for people to accept and see themselves for who they truly are. Being afraid of discovering your true self because you may not like what you find is much worse than whatever you may discover. You can always use the Akashic Records to attract the change you deem necessary for your personal happiness and joy.

Be prepared to discover within you a whole new world, accessible through the Akashic Records. There is more to you than you may ever have thought. Many people spend years thinking that what is on the surface is all there is to explore. The great depths of our souls and energy are way more intriguing and interesting than the surface, with limitless variations. Allow yourself to accept the truth provided to you by the Akashic Records and take hold of your destiny.

Chapter One: The History of the Akashic Records

What Are the Akashic Records?

When starting your spiritual journey, you need to have enough information to be in the right mindset. You need to quench your curiosity about the things you have long thought were beyond your understanding, and it does not help that there is little information that can be found on the Akashic Records. This is why you need to turn to professionals who have already acquired enough knowledge about the Records to guide you. The Akashic Records are based on faith, so you need to open yourself to this experience and let go of your doubts.

The word "Akashic" is an adjective derived from the word Akasha. In Sanskrit, the liturgical language of Hinduism, "Akasha," has various meanings. Some of its shades of meanings include "space," "ancient matter," and "heavens." However, these words do not tell us much about the nature of the Akashic Records. Put simply, the Akashic Records include every thought, intent, and deed that ever occurred in human history. It encompasses the records of other realities and dimensions. Every soul has its own records, in which its past, present, and possible future are inscribed. It is worth mentioning that the records of each individual change as they develop. Although they include future possibilities, Akashic Records do not function like a fortune teller. The possibilities depicted in the Records only allude to people's choices. So, if you have ever wondered if you have a choice on how your life unfolds, be assured that the answer is yes—only your own choices shape your future. The Records are only there to help you reach a favorable outcome. Just think of the Akashic Records as a grand library that contains all the knowledge you need to better your life and reach harmony.

The Akashic Records contain vast knowledge about every occurrence in human history. That is why you can think of them as the records of humanity itself. Since the dawn of time, the Records have been presented to keep track of every source of life, including animals. They record every emotion you have ever felt, every thought that has ever crossed your mind, and every decision you have ever made. Yet, that does not mean that the Records judge your choices or shortcomings as a human. They are only there to record your journey, to aid you, and help you to have a more gratifying experience as a human. The Akashic Records are based on a very interesting concept—the concept of reincarnation. To fully use the Records, you need to believe in that principle. Our world consists of perpetual cycles of death and rebirth. When you die, your soul, which has a specific vibration and essence, is reborn. The Akashic Records have inscriptions of your past lives too. By accessing them, you can learn of your past identity and make use of the experiences from your previous lives.

The Records have two main parts: a stagnant part and a developing one. The stagnant part refers to the essential design of the soul. Think of this design as the perfect state in which someone's soul can exist. The other part, the developing one, records all the lives the soul has gone through. During these lives, the soul wakes up or learns of its genuine uniqueness. In this process, the soul can finally make sense of its essential design and find peace and tranquility. Therefore, reincarnation pertains to the Akashic Records.

You might be wondering where the Akashic Records are stored. This is a valid question that shows your willingness to believe in the Records and benefit from them. To answer your question, the Akashic Records are thought to exist in an ethereal, non-physical plane known as the "Akasha." The Akasha flows through everything in our universe. It flows through nature, matter, and our souls. The Akasha is somewhat like the Force in Star Wars; it encompasses everything. However, the key difference between the two is that the Records do not give you any physical power like telekinesis. The power the Akasha Records gives you is much subtler and understated. They give you a mental and spiritual power to forge your path and find your essential design—to tune your soul to reach its most perfect state.

This begs the question; should you have special powers to access the Akashic Records? The short answer is no—you do not have to be a psychic to access your records. In the past, the Akashic Records were only accessed by shamans, psychics, and some philosophers—people highly attuned to their souls either through psychic powers or plain faith. However, this has greatly changed. In the past few years, there has been a surge in the number of people able to access their records and make use of them. This might be attributed to the state of consciousness that humanity has recently reached. We have become more attuned to our souls, so accessing the Records now is not as hard as it used to be 100 years ago.

Some people think that accessing the Akashic Records can be done only when they are not fully conscious. Some claim they accessed their records in dreams or when they were not conscious. Others point out that they accessed theirs through meditation or a deep trance, both of which involve a state of semi-consciousness. Some say that having a near-death experience is the only way to access the Akashic Records. Yet, this is too extreme and rather unnecessary. You do not have to be on the verge of death to access your records. They are yours, which makes them your birthright. You never have to put yourself in unnecessary danger to read them. Yoga, meditation, and other similar techniques may help you reach a deep state of focus and tranquility. One of the most potent methods used to access the Akashic Records is the Sacred Mayan Prayer. Although the Sacred Prayer can help, it is not sufficient on its own. Opening yourself to the experience and being willing to believe are key to successfully accessing the Akashic Records.

The History of the Akashic Records

Something as potent as the Akashic Records can never stay undetected for long. We can find evidence and various mentions of the Records that date back to ancient civilizations. Records have become a key player in many cultures and societies. However, because the Akashic Records are sometimes referenced to by an array of other names, it's hard to deduce that all those names actually refer to the same concept–the Akashic Records. Despite what some might think, the Records do not oppose or contradict any religion. The Akashic Records are not a religion on their own. We can find mentions of the Records in Hinduism and even Christianity.

In Ancient Egypt

The ancient Egyptian civilization was perhaps one of the first civilizations to mention the concept of the Akashic Records. Evidence of this belief can be easily found in ancient scrolls and texts encoded in hieroglyphs. By discovering those scrolls and decoding them, we can understand how the ancient Egyptians perceived the Akashic Records. The scrolls mention that the priests, or people who could tap into spiritual power, accessed and read their records. Not only that, but they also read the records of others. Of course, that put them in high regard; they were greatly revered by everyone, and even pharaohs sought their counsel. They also interpreted dreams based on the knowledge they gained from the Records. Even ordinary people, who could not read the Records, believed in their existence. The goddess, Seshat, was known as the "Keeper of the Library" or the "Keeper of the Great Book of Souls." Ancient Egyptians also called the Akashic Records the "Repository of Thoth."

In Ancient India

Just like ancient Egyptians, the ancient Indian sages of the Himalayas believed in the existence of the Akashic Records. They believed that every soul had its own records in which its whole life was depicted. They also thought that if people could focus enough, they could access the records and read them. This belief has extended to today's readings of palm leaves. Palm readers believe those leaves include parts of the Akashic Records and that everyone has a specific leaf on which parts of their Records can be seen. According to the beliefs of Hindu mysticism, the Akasha represents the material used to record deeds, thoughts, paths, and emotions. It is thought that Akasha is also an essential component of natural elements, such as air, water, and fire. In this sense, the Akasha encompasses everything, keeping all elements connected and in sync.

In Mayan Culture

The Akashic Records was an open secret in the Mayan culture. Even regular people knew of the records. Those who were able to read them, the high priests and priestesses, shared the knowledge they gained from the Akashic Records with other people to help them forge their path and reach a higher level of knowledge and serenity. Perhaps one of the greatest contributions the Mayans made in connection to the Akashic Records was their creation of the Sacred Prayer. The Sacred Prayer helps anyone access and benefit from the records if they are in a deep state of focus and spiritual attunement.

In Western Culture

Eastern civilizations and cultures are not the only sources of information on the Akashic Records. Western culture caught up around the 16th century. The famous seer, astrologer, and physician, Michel de Nostredame, or Nostradamus, wrote mysterious verses of poetry that predicted future events. He even predicted the Great Chicago Fire of 1871 and the September 11th attacks. It is often thought that he might have accessed the Akasha Records by employing means that stem from Greek visions and Sufi mysticism. One of the first explicit mentions of the Records in western societies was in the late 19th century. The Russian occultist, thinker, and writer Helena Petrovna Blavatsky said that Akasha could create much energy, whether physical or otherwise. Rudolf Steiner, the known Austrian clairvoyant and philosopher, maintained that people could go beyond the material realm to gain more truth and knowledge about themselves. Perhaps the greatest proponent of the Akashic Records was Edgar Cayce, who was known as the Sleeping Prophet. He held many sessions where he answered people's questions and offered them suggestions to heal based on his access to the Akashic Records. Contrary to other beliefs, he thought that the Akashic Records were found on Earth. He proposed that people were ready to make use of the records and forge their destiny. Interestingly, during one of his sessions, the Records revealed that he would fall sick if he continued his readings. He did not heed the warning and died just a year later.

In Religious Contexts

In Christianity and Judaism

The Akashic Records are mentioned under different names in Judaism and Christianity. They are called either the Book of Remembrance or the Book of the Living. Mentioned in the Book of Revelation and the Hebrew Bible, the book of the Living is used to record the names of people who have forged a righteous path for themselves. Those whose names are found in the book are spared from the last judgment. The Book of the Living is mentioned at least six times in the Book of Revelation.

In Islam

The Akashic Records in Islam are known as the Book of Decrees or Preserved Tablet. The Preserved Tablet includes all the thoughts, events, and intents that have ever existed since the dawn of time. The core difference between Islam's interpretation and other interpretations of the Akashic Records is the belief that everyone has an angel who records their deeds. According to this belief, an angel is assigned to every individual and follows them, recording everything they do.

The Benefits of Reading the Akashic Records

After this healthy dose of history and general information on the Akashic Records, you may now wonder about how they can benefit you. Well, accessing and reading the Akashic Records can prove to be a life-transforming experience. The vast knowledge found in the Records can point you in the right direction and give your life a much-needed purpose. Here are some merits of accessing your Akashic Records:

Learning from Your Past Lives

We have established that the concept of reincarnation is closely tied to the Akashic Records. The Records depict your soul's entire history, including your past lives. It is natural to be curious about who you were in your past lives, as such a discovery can help you know who you are now. By reading your Akashic Records, you can learn more about yourself and find your life's purpose. Also, some aspects of your past lives might be affecting your current one. For example, you might have been plagued by poverty in a previous life, and that poverty is now an aspect of your current one. In a similar vein, certain phobias that seem to have no known source or triggers can be a sign of a problem in one of your previous lives. By identifying what is blocking you from having a fuller, richer experience, you can clear these blocks and feel more self-assured.

Getting Definitive Answers to Your Questions

Perpetual curiosity is a big part of the human experience. We questioned, doubted, and searched for answers. However, finding definitive answers to your big questions can prove difficult. After all, you are a mortal who does not possess vast, divine knowledge. What if I told you that you could tap into that knowledge and get answers to your burning questions and more? Accessing and reading the Akashic Records can be just the thing you need. You can learn from the Masters and Teachers of the Records about the secrets of the universe and finally find the peace you have always yearned to feel.

Gaining More Confidence

All humans experience moments when negative thoughts dominate their lives. This natural yet scary part of existence can hamper your plans and make you doubt yourself. These moments of self-doubt can cause you to underestimate yourself or even quit the activities you are most passionate about. Because we need reassurance occasionally, we need to trust in something bigger than ourselves—something that holds all knowledge. The Akashic Records can help reassure you of your worth and talents. The confirmation the Records provide might enable you to go on with your life and identify your soul's essential design. Not only will this enhance your quality of life, but it will also help you make informed decisions based on your soul's identity and talents.

Having a Sanctuary

We all dream of having a safe space, a refuge, or a sanctuary where we can have all the time in the world to reflect and grow. Akashic Records offer the perfect place to do so. They are, in themselves, a sanctuary where you can just take a few minutes to relax and forget about your everyday worries. Nothing is hurried in the Records; you are not tied to someone else's schedule. It is a place where the concepts of time and space disappear, allowing you an organic reflecting experience through which you can know who you are and who you will be. This is perhaps why many people who have accessed the Akashic Records return to them multiple times a day for meditation and reflection. It is a place only governed by serenity and knowledge.

Getting a Glimpse of Future Possibilities

This is where the potential of the Akashic Records shines. Because the Records contain information about the past, present, and future, it includes all the possible paths your soul can take. Accessing and reading your Akashic Records can offer an enlightening experience. Instead of wondering about the future, with all its vagueness and unknown paths, you can have all the possibilities stretched out before your eyes. The Akashic Records do not function as a crystal ball that shows you your future, as only you can shape your destiny. But the knowledge they encompass can help you create the outcome you want based on your informed choices. For instance, Edgar Cayce could have stepped back from his Akashic readings to avoid health issues, yet he chose not to. The possibilities the Records show you are just events that might occur according to what you choose. The insights they offer are informative, nonetheless.

Improving Your Relationships

Sometimes, we just wish we knew more about how we could improve our relationships. If you are one of the people who find it hard to form and maintain human connections, reading your records can help you overcome this problem. By gaining information about your past lives, you can identify what is blocking you from having healthy relationships, healing and forgive rather than flood yourself with negativity. And you can gain more insights about your loved ones, which will greatly help you improve your relationship with them.

Experiencing True Bliss

The Akashic Records exude an immense amount of light, and such light can feel heady to average humans. Just by standing at the gateways of the Akashic Records, you can get a glimpse of this light, entering a state of full rapture. This state occurs due to the amount of divine energy you are subjected to when you read your records. During this process, you should feel more in sync with your soul and the divine nature that surrounds you.

Chapter Two: Common Myths and Misconceptions

Some common myths and misconceptions surround Akashic Records and are mainly driven by a lack of knowledge. In this chapter, we will discuss these myths in detail and why people should embrace Akashic records for their moral, spiritual, and psychological fulfillment.

Common Myths About Akashic Records

As you have read in the previous chapter, Akashic Records consist of a record of what has happened, what is happening, and what will happen. These are powerful and intuitive tools, comprised of life-changing information that can help readers connect with various records. According to the records, time is flat, and something that happened many years back could also happen to you today or tomorrow.

Everything has its Akashic Record, which can also be called "A Book of Life." However, certain myths embody some beliefs, and some misconceptions are mistaken and wrong with Akashic Records. Different myths and misconceptions overlap sometimes; hence the two terms will be used interchangeably in this chapter.

Only a Few Can Understand and Interpret Akashic Records

The greatest myth surrounding the Akashic Records is that only a select few individuals who are "holier-than-thou" are anointed by God to understand the Records. According to this myth, Records can be understood by a few people gifted with the talent of interpreting them to others. This myth is based on self-worth, where other people often want to view themselves as better than others. This myth posits to the effect that if you are not chosen, then you are not worthy.

The truth about this myth is that we all have an Akashic Record that has been part of our lives for a very long time. The Record originates from the same source that all others do, showing we all come from the same energy. Therefore, since we are all complete and have access to get all the things we need, if we choose carefully, we are more or less the same. No people are more worthy than others. To dispel this myth, the counterargument heavily draws from equality, which states we are all equal before God. This makes it possible for everyone to understand the meaning of Records without seeking assistance from the "chosen ones."

Humans Should not Access Akashic Records During their Lifetime

There is also a false belief which states that humans should not access Akashic Records during their lifetime. The myth says that humans have only the privilege to peer inside the Records when they die. A closer analysis of this myth shows it does not make sense since it defies logic for the source to create records about our actions, deeds, thoughts, and other information about our lifetime only to be used when we are dead.

The purpose of the information stored in the Records is that it should be applied to our life so it can help us make informed, life-changing decisions. Records should help us learn and master different skills and techniques that can improve our lives instead of accessing that information only when we are dead. We are provided with the tools that can help us make aligned and appropriate decisions throughout our lives instead of waiting to die first and then applying that knowledge. Likewise, we live once, therefore, so we should use the knowledge that we acquire to improve our lives.

People Seek Answers to the Future from Akashic Records

This is a misconception that purports that people can ask the Records for answers about the future. Sometimes, the answers you will get do not necessarily come to fruition as suggested or described by the Records. When you consult Akashic Records for answers, you should always remember that you are the master of your destiny. Thus, you should be in control of your life and know that the Records are there to tell you the most likely outcome of something based on the trajectory of events you are already within.

The records are not synonymous with prophecy, but they just act as guidelines that can help you decide based on the outcome of a similar situation that has happened. The same trajectory can also happen, and you can use it to create your new path. However, you can use the Records to redirect your possible outcomes from a specific scenario rather than depending on the Records to provide you answers. The records are effective because they help you project the likely outcome of something based on experience. Here, it is the experience that can help you deduce probable answers from the things yet to occur.

Akashic Records are Used to Control People

Another misconception is that Akashic Records are a form of mystery used to control people. In other sectors of different societies, these records are viewed as a cult controlled by sects and religions to have power over other people. Certain religions seek to control other people so they can gain power and make more money, but Akashic Records are not like these sects. These are records that can be relied on for life-changing purposes and other related needs.

Therefore, if you use the Records for spiritual, moral, and psychological guidance, then no one can control you. The only person who can control you is the one whom you permit to do so. For instance, if you join a religious cult, you are effectively giving the leaders some power to control you. Otherwise, you are fully in control of your life, and no one else can control you if you do not allow it. Akashic Records present the users with the opportunity to make personal choices in life with no undue influence from other people.

Accessing the Akashic Records will Tamper with the Soul Blueprint

Some people believe that they are not allowed to access the Akashic Records because they will tamper with their soul blueprint. According to this myth, the guide gives you the soul blueprint that can lead to the implosion of the whole world if you tamper with it. However, there is no reason you should deprive yourself of access to something that is already written or recorded. There is a purpose for anything that is written, and the Records are no exception. It is the living who can read so we can see that the Records are specifically meant for us to be read.

You can choose your path in consultation with your guides who have a responsibility to guide you in your path towards the growth of the soul. The guides are only there to help you, and there is no judgment or any hierarchy that can scare you. You can get as much support as you want from the guide since you have free will. When you access your Records, your reality will not be compromised. Everything will be joyful and fun as you learn. Information is not cast in stone and you have the power and will to change it so it can suit your needs.

You can choose the information you want, which will help create the best life for yourself. You can get help from others, while you choose the information that has true meaning to your life. Thus, accessing information from the Records will not tamper with your soul blueprint but, instead, gives you its power and strength so you can realize your goals and aspirations.

I am not Gifted Enough to Access Records

This myth emanates from the inferiority complex among different people. Whereas everyone can access the Records, there is someone who is saying that they are not gifted to do the same. The question is, says who? You should also ask yourself why you feel that you are less than what you are worth. The belief that you hold for yourself can make you feel that you are not gifted to access Records, but the truth of the matter is that this has nothing to do with the records. Some people lack self-confidence, and these are the people who believe that certain things are impossible.

Accessing your Records should be a matter of personal choice, and nothing can stop you. This helps you to identify your talents and divine gifts, which require belief and a willingness to allow the connection. To create this connection, people need to work on the relationship. Your willingness to be connected will determine your connection with your Records. The primary thing you should work on is overcoming an inferiority complex that can make you feel you are not gifted. Only then will you be able to access your Records and change your life.

A positive attitude leads to behavior change, which, in turn, can shape your perceptions and world view. Some people simply believe that they cannot do something because of fear. Instead of thinking you are not gifted enough to access the Records, you need to have a positive attitude. To overcome the fear of the unknown, you should give remind yourself that nothing is impossible.

I am Afraid Of Hearing Negative Things About Myself

It is natural to have this kind of negative intuition about yourself, but the truth is that you are not as bad as you think. Some people fear opening their Records for fear of hearing bad things about their past and their contributions to the world. This fear factor is mainly induced by a lack of self-confidence, and this has contributed to the downfall of many people. All the same, you should know that every person has a purpose on this planet, and your contribution cannot be like every individual. The fact that you matter should help you overcome the negative perceptions that you may have about yourself.

Records mainly focus on love and truth. These two components play a pivotal role in shaping our integrity and how we relate with others in society. Therefore, you should accept your personality and remember that Records are done out of love to help you realize weaknesses so that you can clear them. The Records are also aimed at giving you the power to create a pleasant path where you choose right over wrong. Essentially, we all aim to be righteous, and this can be achieved if we are in a position to learn from previous mistakes so that we avoid following the same path again.

The judgment about self is outdated since it can only slide you more into shame. When you ask questions of the Records, you should not always expect positive comments. In real life, constructive criticism is vital since it helps us to realize where we are lacking. When you know your weaknesses, you are in a better position to improve yourself and become a better person.

Akashic Records Can Provide Information to Solve Problems Immediately

There is also a false belief among people that Akashic Records can provide specific information to help the user to immediately solve problems. In one way or the other, every person experiences confusion as well as frustration with life such that they seek divine intervention to overcome the challenges. Some people believe that if they turn to the Records, they can get immediate answers that can solve their problems.

Indeed, you will get support and answers to the questions and problems you are experiencing in life, but you should not expect everything to be sudden. The purpose of Akashi Records is to help you self-introspect so that you can get the truth of what you want from yourself. You can bring your questions to the Records, and what you should expect to get is not a rapid response but guidance that can help you overcome the challenges that you are be facing.

The response that you will get helps to open your heart and soul to other alternatives that can help you resolve the challenges that you are facing. There are different problem-solving strategies that you should apply to get long-lasting solutions to the challenges that you may be experiencing at any given time. While you can get the assistance that can help you solve different problems, the ultimate solutions come from your heart, which knows what is good for you.

Can Akashic Records Make my Future Great?

Akashic Records are specifically concerned about your intuition now, and there is often a false belief that they can predict your future and make it great. The records have nothing to do with acquiring unique skills that can transform your future, but they simply help you learn to trust yourself. Lack of trust is the major contributor to failure among people. Therefore, trusting yourself is a major stride towards the attainment of your desired goals in life.

Records do not expand your psychic abilities. They can only help you cope with fear, while at the same time realizing the disbelief within you that can impact your desire to live happily. Records can help you to open up to any opportunity that comes your way. Records are also amazing in that they help create self-awareness about different things that can affect your life. Since the Records constitute spiritual practice, you should use them to seek guidance so that you can pursue your dreams with confidence. To be on the right track, you should show some willingness to change your mind so that you can have a different world view.

As you have observed above, Akashic Records are an amazing tool that can be used by anyone with an open mind. You can open the records and ask anything about your life. Records can uplift your soul to another level, especially when you discover the hidden truth about your personality. They are life-changing, and they can help you shape your destiny. Indeed, none but ourselves can determine our destinies, so Akashic Records are the best good starting point if you want to achieve greatness in your life.

Chapter Three: The Eternal Timeline

As explained in the previous chapter, the Akashic Records contain every thought, intent, or emotion you have ever felt in this life or your previous ones. The Records also contain possible future outcomes, which is why you may be tempted to access and read your Records. The Akashic Records of the past, present, and future create what is known as the "eternal timeline." This timeline can be easily traveled through the Pathway Prayer Process. However, before learning how you can access the records, you must know the distinction between past, present, and future records.

Past Records

Your soul might choose to be reincarnated for many reasons. Some just want to fix some of the mistakes and patterns of their previous lives, while others want to come to enjoy the bliss that life experiences can offer. It requires many reincarnations to reach your soul's essential design or most perfect state. Nonetheless, your willingness to open your records shows that this life might be the turning point for you. Indubitably, your past lives can affect your current one through your recorded karma. In Sanskrit, the word usually means "deed" or "action," but karma usually goes beyond that. It encompasses your thoughts and emotions too. Traumatic experiences or negative thoughts and emotions can create blocks in our current lives. This, of course, can prevent us from enjoying our lives to the fullest. So, many people seek to open their past records to identify the source of the problems they are facing. Yet, first, you need to investigate present life clues that point to the possibility that your past lives are impacting you now.

Look at your current patterns of behavior. Usually, current patterns are a result of old ones. For example, if you cannot seem to shoulder the responsibility of your work and jump from one job to the next every few months, this could indicate that you had issues with stability and responsibility in your past lives. This also applies to addictions and negative thought patterns. Often, people who are plagued with negative thoughts, or immerse themselves in negative patterns, have destructive past life patterns that reoccur. To put a stop to such patterns, you need to open your past records to find the root of the problem.

Similarly, chronic physical or medical problems, like arthritis, can signal past life traumatic events or accidents. For instance, if you are suffering from chronic pain that refuses to be cured, no matter how many treatments you get, you may discover that it is the result of a severe injury you sustained in one of your past lives. Your financial situation can also be influenced by your past lives. By investigating the patterns of poverty dominating your life and accessing your records, you might be surprised to discover that you suffered from the same circumstances before and that the pattern is just repeating itself.

Another aspect that many are interested in investigating is their relationship problems. Unfortunately, not everyone has it easy; some cannot form or sustain any meaningful relationships. If you are one of those people, rest assured that there is nothing wrong with you. Past karma can be a plausible cause for your dissatisfaction when it comes to personal relationships. The thoughts we feed ourselves make up the energy that flows to the

Akashic Records and inscribes your development. Your past self might have focused on negative thoughts about love. They might have felt that they were unworthy of it or that it was a source of weakness. Those thoughts are now recorded in your past records and continue to influence your current relationships. However, there is no reason to fret, as you can fix the problem by uprooting its cause.

It is easy to misunderstand how karma works in the context of the Akashic Records, but you must know that it does not refer to judgment or punishment. It is simply a record of how your past lives were lived. In fact, your past records contain millions of positive experiences that you can learn from. Even traumatic incidents and experiences provide a great chance of growing and reaching your soul's most perfect state. There are three reasons for karma: repetition, retribution, and compensation. Repetition refers to a behavior pattern that keeps recurring. However, every time it does, it becomes more dangerous. For instance, if someone had minor problems with overeating in one life, such a pattern may be repeated in their current one, causing more severe results like eating disorders. Retribution, on the other hand, refers to negative or difficult past relationships. Negative aspects of relationships like abuse and mistrust in a past life might create a pattern that perpetuates and impacts your present relationships. Finally, compensation refers to things you lacked in your previous lives and are trying to compensate for in this one. This compensation can, nonetheless, be dangerous. If you were poor in a previous life, you might compensate for this now by overspending. Certainly, overspending is negative compensation and a pattern you need to eliminate from your life.

So, how can you fix something that has already been recorded? Well, the process is called "rewriting your past records." However impossible this may sound, you need to know that you have full control over your records and can rewrite your past ones once you gain enough enlightenment. You need to start by focusing on the one aspect you want to view. For example, you can focus on your relationship issues. Your Akashic Records will then let you view the past event that led to your problems. Now, by viewing and understanding that experience, you can rewrite it. To do that, envision a better conclusion to the situation. Let's say that you cannot find a partner now. By viewing your past records, you may discover that you had a difficult relationship with your spouse in one of your past lives. You can then change the outcome of this relationship by envisioning that you started listening to each other more and fixed your marriage. Doing that should remove the blockage you have been suffering from and allow you to pursue healthy relationships.

Present Records

While accessing your past records can help you heal and remove blockages from your life, reading your present Akashic Records has many more benefits. Every moment is recorded in detail in the records, and your soul is always vibrating and providing your records with enough energy to inscribe everything. What does that mean? It means that your current behavior, thought processes, and emotions are continuously recorded and will most certainly affect you in the future. By the time you read your past records in one of your next lives, your current choices will have led to either a satisfactory life or a lacking one. This is why it is extremely important to control yourself and enforce positive thoughts and emotions.

Identifying Current Patterns of Negative Behavior

Opening your present Akashic Records can shed light on your current patterns of behavior. It can show you both your positive and negative patterns. Although you cannot exactly rewrite your present records because they are always changing, you can change your behavior in real life. In this sense, the Akashic Records are only there to help you recognize destructive patterns and fix them. For instance, you might be struggling with alcoholism and remain oblivious to the fact that it has become a real problem. Your present records can help you see this from a different perspective, allowing you to finally acknowledge that you indeed have a problem. You can then use this knowledge to better your life and enhance your soul's vibrations.

Identifying Patterns of Negative Thoughts and Emotions

You are the sole entity responsible for your happiness, and you are the only one who can choose to live happily. In this spirit, your current thoughts and emotions have a big impact on your future. The way you perceive yourself is of utmost importance. If you are always having negative or self-deprecating thoughts, you can open your present records to investigate the problem and find more clarity on the issue. We are not going to advocate the power of positive thinking because it has already been proven effective, but you really need to assert your self-worth and boost your self-esteem if you want to change your life. Because the Akashic Records are very sensitive to everything we think, feel, or do, we need to always think positively, even when faced with difficult situations. For example, choosing to focus only on the worst aspects of your job is bound to be inscribed in your records and may even cause problems during your next reincarnation. Instead, you can focus on its positive aspects, whether that is an experience or monetary gain. When assigned a difficult task, instead of thinking, "I can't finish this," you can say to yourself, "It is certainly a difficult task, but I am sure I can do it." Apply this to every aspect of your life, and you will reap amazing benefits.

Identifying Negative Spiritual Patterns

Your spirit may be encumbered by the difficulties you are facing or the everyday worries you must deal with. However, this does not mean that there is no way to fix this. To combat this, you must focus on your negative patterns of behavior, thoughts, and emotions, using the previous points for guidance. By doing that, you will be effectively healing your soul and helping it transcend old worries and grievances. This, in turn, will increase your soul's vibrations and help it reach its divine ideal faster. In the long run, this process will unlock many worthwhile future opportunities that you would not be able to make use of otherwise. Acknowledging that everything you do can affect your future, as well as the next reincarnations, can help you adopt a new outlook on life, helping you indulge in fresh experiences and utilize positive thinking to your advantage.

Future Records

Akashic Records open up a world of possibilities, as you can use them to gain more foresight about the future. A lot of people think that accessing their future records is dangerous because they might risk seeing something bad happening to them down the line. They prefer to stay blind to their future. The experience of seeing your future, while hard, can be truly enlightening. You cannot get this information elsewhere, and by remembering that your records are essentially your birthright, you can understand that they mean you no harm; they are only there to guide you to your divine ideal. Nonetheless, because your soul's energy and vibrations are writing your present records now, your future records are ever-changing. Nothing is set in stone, and this realization might put you at ease. Even if you end up seeing an unfavorable outcome, it does not necessarily mean that whatever you have seen will take place. All you can see by accessing your future records are mere possibilities until you decide to act on them.

Using Future Records to Fix Present Problems

Getting a glimpse of the future is not a means of tormenting yourself. Although seeing a traumatic event down the line is certainly dispiriting, the Akashic Records are just trying to nudge you in the right direction. They are giving you the chance to change your destiny. The possibilities you can see now are merely a reflection of your current choices and actions. They are the most logical outcomes that can stem from your present behavior. For example, if you have been recently overworking yourself, one of your future possibilities might include health or relationship problems due to your busy schedule. The Records will alert you to this and help you find the root of the problem. Through this process, you can identify negative current patterns that you might have been previously unaware of. This way, you can take active steps to eliminate such patterns and change future outcomes.

Revisiting Your Future Records

As you change your current patterns of thoughts, behavior, and emotions, your future Akashic Records will change too. As we have previously mentioned, the future records reflect your current actions. So, it makes sense to revisit them occasionally, to gauge the way your future will shape up to be, based on the new changes you have implemented. Of course, if you have made a drastic change, your future records will be greatly altered. You might even notice that some scenarios have disappeared completely and been replaced with new, more positive ones. Yet, if you cannot sense a big change in your future records, you need to give yourself time. Sometimes, changes take a while to affect your life. Although your future records may seem stagnant now, rest assured that they are just waiting for the change to take effect. So, try to check your future Akashic Records as often as possible to see all the new possibilities recently added to your records.

The Pathway Prayer Process

The Pathway Prayer is a means of accessing the Akashic Records. It was developed by Linda Howe, who holds a Ph.D. in spiritual studies and is the founder of the Linda Howe Center for Akashic Studies that was established to encourage using the Akashic Records for empowerment. Considered the most effective and simplest method of accessing one's records, the Pathway Prayer is very easy to use, which makes it great for beginners who want to consult the wisdom of the Records. What also makes this method very potent is that it can work when you want to read your own records or someone else's. So, this layer of versatility is certainly appreciated. The Pathway Prayer has two parts: an opening prayer and a closing one. The opening prayer consists of requesting the direction and guidance of the Masters of the records, the Teachers, and the Loved Ones. In the closing prayer, you thank the Akashic

Records for the provided insight. Most importantly, you need to use your legal name when chanting the opening prayer. The third paragraph should be repeated thrice. The first time, you need to use the personal pronouns "me" and "myself." In the second and third time, make sure to use your legal name instead of the personal pronouns highlighted between brackets. According to Linda Howe (2009), the text of the Pathway Prayer is as follows:

Opening Prayer

And so, we do acknowledge the Forces of Light
Asking for guidance, direction, and courage to know the Truth
As it is revealed for our highest good and the highest good of Everyone connected to us.
Oh, Holy Spirit of God,
Protect me from all forms of self-centeredness
And direct my attention to the work at hand.
Help me to know (myself) in the Light of the Akashic Records,
To see (myself) through the eyes of the Lords of the Records,
And enable me to share the wisdom and compassion that the Masters, Teachers, and Loved Ones of (me) have for (me).
The Records are now open.

Closing Prayer

I would like to thank the Masters, Teachers, and Loved Ones for their love and compassion.
I would like to thank the Lords of the Akashic Records for their point of view.
And I would like to thank the Holy Spirit of Light for all knowledge and healing.
The Records are now closed. Amen.
The Records are now closed. Amen.
The Records are now closed. Amen. (p. 165)

Chapter Four: Past Lives

Beyond the physical actions that contribute to our existence, have you often pondered a more intricate explanation of how we came about as human beings? Perhaps it's the innate curiosity of the human mind and the belief that there must be something more to our being other than the hard facts that we know about the cycle of life. We are born, we go unknowingly through a life filled with a myriad of possibilities until we eventually perish. Simple truths that no one, no matter their beliefs, can dare to challenge. However, to some, the idea of this isolated existence in which every human walks their own path in life alone does not seem convincing enough. They believe the realm of spirits to be far more connected than what our earthly minds could possibly understand.

Many eastern religions that originated in Asia, like Hinduism and Buddhism, are based on the dichotomy of body and soul. Just because a person dies does not mean that their soul follows; instead, it continues in some other form or shape. Building on the concept of soul continuity, modern religions emerged, such as Theosophy, which was established in New York in the United States sometimes during the late nineteenth century.

Theosophy, and other later religions, teach that every single human thought, action, or feeling that takes place on earth, whether good or bad, is recorded in a metaphysical memory system known as the Akashic Records. Beyond merely keeping records of the aggregate doings of mankind, the Akashic records are thought to have an immense effect on the way we live our lives, our relationships, and the kind of future we attract. Those who subscribe to the validity of the Akashic Records argue that accessing one's records can divulge information about their past lives, hoping that it might help them to have more control over their destiny, based on the lives they are leading.

Accessing the records is no longer exclusive to certain individuals; regular people can seek guidance to do so on their own. In this chapter, we are going to focus on exploring past lives through the Akashic Records. So, if this is your first time reading about the records, remember to keep an open mind to get the most out of your reading.

The Significance of Past Lives in the Akashic Records

Based on the belief that the human soul is indefinite, and that the Akashic Records holds data about what has been, is, and will be, you can learn about your own past lives through accessing the records. Getting to know about your own soul's past, where it has been, and the lives it held can help you identify why you have certain feelings, or how you cultivated specific behaviors. You must have heard the saying that you cannot know where you are going unless you understand where you came from; by allowing you a peek through the past, the Akashic Records can help you to go through life with more conviction. To put it in a more romanticized manner, past lives are the chance for your soul to get it right.

By living multiple lives, your soul is on an eternal journey to continuously improve until it can finally reach a state of higher being. Buddha himself is believed to have had close to a thousand lives before he reached enlightenment. This underlying glorification of redemption is not foreign to all earthly religions known to us humans. When it comes to matters of the soul, nothing is absolute. Maybe it is our egos that initiated the idea of the continuity of our souls, our own rejection of the possibility of being done, and stopping to exist once and for all. The idea of past lives, however, references fluidity and a kind of immortality that surpasses our physical bodies.

Does Everyone Have Past Lives?

This must be one of the first questions that crossed your mind when you first heard about the Akashic Records. You must have heard about the theories of reincarnation and how many people strongly believe that they used to be someone else in a past life. Although you might think that such people have an exclusive connection with other worlds, if you pay closer attention, you can find tons of rather tangible clues that support the validity of this claim. Think about the feeling of familiarity that you experience when you meet some people for the first time. Why do you think you seem to "connect" without any prior interactions? What about the concept of deja vu? You go to a place you have never seen before and meet people you never knew existed, yet somehow it all feels like a playback of a memory stored somewhere deep in your psyche.

There are never any clear explanations about these unnatural phenomena, no matter how they are commonly dismissed as mystic occurrences. Furthermore, the special bond you have with another person, or affinity towards a place, is more evidence that your soul has already met or visited them before in another life. It is not an easy thing to wrap your head around if you haven't been down that road before, where you choose to entertain your inquisitive mind. However, when you buy into the idea that everything holds a meaning, you can discover a lot by simply opening your eyes and preparing your senses to analyze what is happening around you.

Akashic Past Life Readings

Now that you understand more about the theory of past lives, and how you can benefit from such knowledge, you must know what to expect from Akashic past life readings. Maybe you are at a point in your life where you feel so overwhelmed by the noise around you that you decide it is time to look into yourself. Many people waste so much time trying to control circumstances and outward events that they do not have any power over, and only a few reach the realization that all they must do is focus on themselves. Seeking to access the Akashic Records is a way of adopting the notion that your past, present, and future coexist together somewhere that you can reach, to find abundance and good fortune in your life. Once you decide to go through with this plan, you can choose to do a guided quest, as mentioned above, or you can take it upon yourself to request accessing the records. Later, in other chapters of this book, you will be introduced to a step-by-step guide on how to access the Akashic records and have your own reading. However, for now, we want to focus on the role that past lives play in the Akashic readings. Reaching your past lives can be very useful when you are looking for answers that do not exist in your current life, why certain fears are holding you back, or pinpointing some patterns in your relationships with your loved ones. You have the option to visit either:

- Your Most Recent Past Life

This is the life that is closer to our definition of time or to the life you have right now.

- Your Most Significant Past Life

This life is the one that seems to have the greatest effect on your current one. For some reason, the experiences that transpired in that life resonate rather strongly with what you are going through now.

- Your Soul's Past life of Choice

This past life is the one that your soul freely chooses to revisit. You might not get the chance to know why, but if you like, you can come back to it later in future readings to look for answers about this specific past life. As we mentioned earlier, there is a reason and meaning behind everything, so it is always a good idea to dig deeper. It will help you get to know more about yourself and your soul's travels.

Past Life Regression versus Past Life Reading

In past life regressions, you get the chance to experience your past lives in a fuller way by going under the hypnosis of a specialized therapist and get to live vicariously through that period. Although it is more intricate and offers deeper insights, past life regressions are relatively expensive and usually take multiple sessions before they can be fruitful, not to mention having to endure the inconvenience of being hypnotized. Past life readings, on the other hand, give you access to your past lives in an easier way. You might take longer to reach the same depth as with past life regressions; however, to normal people, it is usually enough to put them in contact with their previous lives. Both past life regressions and readings share the same purpose, to help you use the information you uncover in your present life.

Most experienced readers warn their subjects about getting sucked into a past reality and losing their grip on reality, reveling in the what-has-been. They can lose their way in their current life and get caught in a state of limbo where they are neither here nor there. If you are going to attempt either, you must identify your intentions and commit to them and avoid being sidetracked despite the temptations. You must understand that past lives are in no way an alternative to your present life; instead, they allow you to learn from past lessons and make better choices, living a more fulfilled life.

Akashic Records and Karma

To better understand how the Akashic Records tap into past lives, you need to learn about the principles of Karma. In Buddhism and Hinduism, your actions and doings dictate how your life turns out. The good you do will eventually come back to you in this current life, as well as any future ones. This means that any misfortunes you are encountering, or your constant struggles can be due to a karmic consequence of actions that you committed in one of your past lives. People wishing to be relieved from the wrath of Karma resort to the Akashic Records to find what the things are that they need to make right as a form of retaliation. You must be wondering if this means that you are but a spectator to your own life, as your fate is already written, and you only get to "watch" it through some archived records. If that is the truth, then what is it that you are doing here, and what is your purpose?

You must understand that we are free beings, and you have the chance to turn your life around should you wish, and that is what will be mentioned in the Akashic Records. The records are more of an observatory tool, they do not influence your actions and thoughts, but instead, they simply store them. Even if you are still on the fence about the Akashic Records and how real they might or might not be, believing in Karma will serve you well in your life. If every person believed that what they put out into the world will imminently reflect on their own life, humanity would have been saved a whole lot of pain and suffering. Take a moment and entertain this thought, you do not necessarily have to believe in Karma per se, call it what you may, but do yourself a favor and give it the attention it deserves.

What Should You Look For In Past Lives?

Just like your own present life, your past lives are full of many details that lack value or significance. During a past life reading, especially when you are doing it for the first time, you can be flooded with millions of thoughts, feelings, and ideas. If you stop to take notice of each one, your precious reading time will be wasted.

You need to prepare for your reading session. List several issues that you wish to find answers for in the Akashic Records. Limit your inquiries to a few brief open-ended questions until you get more used to the readings. For example, request information about your fear of heights, or the roots of your timid nature. By focusing on specific topics, you will have a better chance of enjoying a more informative reading session. During the reading, apply the basic rules of meditation where you only get to observe irrelevant thoughts and feelings and then let them go without entertaining them. Once you gain enough knowledge to reach the Akashic Records whenever you wish, articulating your queries will become much easier, and you will be able to find what you are looking for every time.

How Your Present Life Will Fare as a Past Life

Given the principles of the Akashic Records that we have discussed, and the characteristics of past lives, you can probably now see the responsibility you have to ensure your present turns into an amiable past for your future self. Unlike in your past lives, you now know enough about the consequences of your beliefs and deeds in this world. So, how can you use this to your future self's benefit? What should you do to get rid of any tensions and unpleasantness that might travel through to your future self? The answer is quite simple; you need to be more conscious. Starting right now, repeat it over and over until thinking, acting, and speaking consciously comes naturally. Think of it as improving the cards that your future self will be dealt. You will be giving yourself a head start by laying a strong foundation of honesty, kindness, and joy.

Choose to lead a good life, be of service to others, and do not lose your way amidst the noise of today's world. Use what you learn in your past life's readings to avoid making the same mistakes that you are trying to fix in your present. Notice what from the past has had the biggest impact and direct all your energy towards making it right for your future self. Although this is a logical progression of using your past lives to only improve your present, not everyone can come to it naturally on their own. That is why it is important to highlight it here so that you can understand how to build on your knowledge of your past lives and carry it forward.

Thinking about your life as an extension of other lives can be so empowering. When the world seems overwhelming, and you feel like you have no idea where you are going, you can always find comfort in knowing that, in a sense, you have been there before, you have figured it out once, and you can do it again. If you are going to walk away with anything from this chapter, be it the fact that you are more than your human mind can possibly fathom. Your life demands and deserves to be respected. So, hold that thought tight as you read on because we are about to get into the practical part of this book. The coming chapters will show you how to apply the theory to find your purpose and heal using the Akashic Records.

Chapter Five: Find Your Purpose

Not every organism longs for a purpose, but almost all organisms find it automatically, except for humans. Trees, for example, exist in their own plane of energy and consciousness, breathing, exhaling, and branching into magnificent shapes. Their energy planes overlap with ours on numerous occasions. But their purpose hardly ever changes. They are always trees. Humans, on the other hand, can easily get lost through overlaps with other planes, organisms, situations, and inner energy. Finding a purpose can sometimes be a rocky and intense ride through various planes of consciousness and vibrations.

What Makes Purpose Important

Before you try to use the Akashic Records to navigate the realms of personal and spiritual purposes, you need to make sure that you know why you're looking for a purpose. When you're using the Akashic Records, you're trying to go deeper into many profound elements of your current life and older ones, and you've come to this plane to transcend and purify. This means that you always have to maintain a constant state of honesty with yourself. There is absolutely no way to find any karmic and truthful purpose without being completely connected to your true self.

Knowing your current and perhaps future purposes will help you stay focused and grounded. You will be able to see the precious elements and forms of energy that matter the most in your life, and many of those elements will begin showing themselves to you through vibrations, karma, or different forms of energy-based revelations. Once you're able to stay focused on one purpose for a long time, the energy intensifies, this simple purpose that you found for yourself suddenly becomes a passion. This burning energy can flow through your body and soul, unshackling you from the restrictions placed on you in past lifetimes.

It's easy to recognize people who have known their purpose for years. They emanate energy and aura to those who are close to them. It's the clarity obtained from the sharpening of their passion and purpose that makes them unstoppable. This kind of clarity isn't just used to advance a career or in learning a new skill, but also having the right kind of synchronized vibrations to see the paths that are most suited for them.

The Personal Records

The Akashic Records contain all the paths, energies, frequencies, purposes, and summation of information that you've learned, not only this life but also other lifetimes. These records are full of infinite vibrations that resonate throughout planes that transcend space and time, expanding the energy of the universe. For people who are looking for a purpose, they'll want to access a specific portion of their Akashic Records to facilitate finding their path. This section is known as Personal Records.

You can think of your Personal Records as an infinitely branching tree that casts branches of the entire previous summations of your previous experience and the energy and information contained in your future. Accessing Personal Records may reveal your past and current influences, in addition to the true direction of your soul on earth. While having a purpose is commonly thought of as consciously having it at the front of your mind, most of the our soul's purposes that compel us are not clear in the conscious plane of thought.

It's these deeper roots of purpose that you're trying to find, those that make you feel like you should wake up in the morning and see what each day has to offer.

The Spiritual Purpose

Among the pursuit of earthly purposes, many forget that the spiritual purpose is essential in their endeavor. It being in the background, people often think that pursuing it is an unnecessary effort. But, the only kind of purpose that can allow you to release yourself from the shackles of guilt and inner turmoil is the spiritual purpose. Without this kind of inner peace and tranquility, your other pursuits and endeavors are bound to have less energy and vibrations that drive you forward in your life.

The spiritual purpose is closely linked with the sense of attachment you have to certain people, places, or memories. Consciously directing it will allow you to finally get rid of the habit of finding yourself in loops of self-loathing and destruction, just as constantly picking at a wound will only make it get worse. Your personal purpose is finely tethered to your spiritual purpose because psychology will always be a non-detachable part of your Personal Records.

The Personal Purpose

The personal purpose is like an infinite river that passes through every small or big experience in your life. You may want to know the kind of career or skill you'll learn, but have you ever thought about the kind of emotional and mental life you'd like to lead? People easily start to have tunnel-vision when they're thinking about their future and the kind of life they want to lead, focusing only on the small, practical aspects instead of the major spiritual and emotional ones. Listening to your soul as it guides you to get rid of the fears and worries holding you back is the easiest way to find your true purpose. If you let the fears of the current and past lifetimes put invisible and subconscious shackles on you, it will be hard to move forward through your personal purpose.

You'll learn how to love yourself and have the courage to finally peek into a future where you don't feel threatened by guilt and worries. Your relationships and love lives are all a part of your personal purpose. You may not notice it, but it's a personal purpose that can dictate how you perceive current and past relationships. It's not the type of relationships that matter, whether it's professional, romantic, or even platonic. What truly matters is how they connect with your personal purpose in this current life. Remember, you're not trying to force your way into the Akashic Records, you're only trying to find a way to listen to what these Records have been talking to you about for thousands of years.

Being Stuck

One of the major obstacles that people face when they're trying to find their purpose and talents is becoming stuck in the past. This is directly related to Karma, which you've probably heard of through your interactions with others or reading about other religions. It seems that Karma is one of the energies that a lot of philosophies and religions hinge on. A lot of people resort to the Akashic Records to remove ancient roots that are grounding them from moving forward. It's impossibly hard to find a true purpose if you keep thinking about the past and let it control you.

The task of shedding your ego may seem quite overwhelming when you think about it at first, but it's no harder than removing the illusions of the past. You need to think about what Karma brings to your doorstep as an opportunity; is it negative emotions? Feeling stuck? Loopy thoughts? They're all potential gates to unraveling what's truly holding you back from being in touch with your true soul. Tapping into the Akashic Records for solutions will help you make interesting shifts in your life. The final goal is to transcend your Karma, eluding what's been hindering you for many lifetimes.

If you're not familiar with Karmic entanglement, it's the sum of all the Karmic connections you have connecting to your Karmic patterns. This entanglement is the accumulation of past experiences through family, nation, tribes, and other patterns that can reflect your past lives' Karma. You need to understand that your personal experiences aren't the only things that affect your Karma; it's actually pretty easy for people to get entangled in Karmic patterns that occurred in the past just through the linkage of their heritage.

Untangling Karma

Feeling like a victim to earthly circumstances isn't going to help you find your purpose. In fact, it will only hinder you as you'll be looking through a very narrow field of vision. Once you feel that your life is completely out of your control, you won't be able to muster the required strength to face your Karma and change your path. There is a very big possibility that what's stopping you is Karmic entanglement produced by your past life. A common problematic effect of karmic entanglement is losing your true self of individuality and independence, as your soul becomes entangled with other big and diverse groups.

This is easily observable when you start looking at people born into certain religions, or those who take on a belief system quickly without thinking about the consequences. They can easily become karmic entangled. Fighting this may seem like a harsh battle, but you'll suddenly feel lighter once you become untangled of the vibrations that are bringing you down, and that will allow you to think from a higher plane that can help you change your perspective.

Once you manage to get into your Akashic Records, specifically the Personal Records, look for karmic entanglements associated with your family, race, belief system, and similar associations. Letting yourself be held down by such associations will only cause you to be upset with yourself, hindering your energy from vibrating properly. You are responsible for what you feel and the energy you produce, so make sure you take into consideration not getting too entangled or absorbed in the lives of others.

The Akashic Records and Negative Emotions

You need to understand that you do not have room to house all the emotions at the same time. This means that when you are in a state of constant fear or worry about certain things, you're taking away a big portion of the space that happiness is supposed to occupy. But, it's also not that simple; this occupation can cause many lingering strands of energy that can affect how you think for a pretty long time. Being constantly stressed and worried takes away from your happiness, but also blocks and incapacitates your ability to be able to identify happiness in the future.

From a medical standpoint, fear and stress can deal a lot of damage to the physiological body. Unfortunately, this kind of damage can find a way to translate and transfer this damage to the soul. This isn't vague advice, telling you to stop being worried, it's never that simple. But you should be conscious of the vibrations and energies that you are allowing your soul to absorb. Your inner energy is not fragile, but it can be molded quickly into something dangerous if you leave it to circumstances.

Akashic Records heavily emphasize our ability to retrieve our divine essence from the shackled constraints we put on it. You may not notice it now, but over time, you'll notice how the connection to a certain story or narrative can cause you to feel unpleasant feelings. And this means that it's actually a choice. You need to be careful not to polarize yourself on such a wide spectrum, and you shouldn't detach yourself from everything to avoid feeling unpleasant feelings. Recognize your emotions and try to find the deeper causes that make you feel such unpleasant feelings. After all, the outcome of those feelings is dependent on how you respond to them.

Reclaiming Power

While you're viewing your Akashic Records, you'll find a lot of ways to respond to information. The key to reclaiming your power is to control how far it affects you. Letting your feelings blow out of proportion means that you are not tackling another issue. The energy that you've been blocking from circulating in your body is disrupting the natural and tranquil rhythm of other frequencies. If you find yourself getting too angry over matters you know very well shouldn't bother you much, then your soul is trying to release a lot of negative energy it has stored for a while.

Once you see your emotions through the Akashic Records, you'll find that it is quite easy to analyze and solve a lot of situations that once gave you a hard time. Your energy shouldn't be zapped suddenly when you face a new problem, as long as you stay conscious and on top of your emotions. Don't let your inner victim take away the power you have to resolve issues. Sadly enough, this inner victim has probably zapped your energy in countless other lifetimes, but once you're able to see through this destructive pattern, you'll be able to balance the situation entirely.

Our society barely gives us time to think and act at our own pace, and this can cause you a lot of problems when dealing with your inner self. Utilize the Akashic Records to access a timeline that can never be affected by others. You'll be able to use your new-gained energy to create joy and whatever you desire in your life. It's pretty common for people to stop in their tracks once they feel victims of circumstances that they are not responsible for, thinking that it's fate or destiny that has forced misfortune upon them. Use the Akashic Records to get out of this destructive loop that keeps you from being able to look forward and regain control of your destiny, instead of being enslaved by it.

The True Depths of Healing

Self-realization is the key that can unlock your healing process. Transcending karmic patterns is the true spiritual purpose that can help you attract joy and other pleasant feelings to your life. It's not easy to avoid being tempted by the webs of illusions that this earthly world offers. This is where self-realization comes into play. It will allow you to go into your Akashic Records to heal the wounds of the past and connect further with your soul. The current narrative could be part of the illusions that plague this world. If you want to follow your true narrative, you'll need to recreate it from the beginning. You'll feel more powerful and in control of your life as you begin to reshape your karmic patterns.

The Akashic Records are going to be your main link to the divine essence within yourself. This bond that you create will keep on providing you with gifts, talents, wisdom, and the power to help others see things for their true nature. While using the Akashic Records isn't the only way to achieve what you desire, it's still the quickest because you'll be healed and unhindered by the illusions of life. Staying focused on your Karma, while viewing your Akashic Records, will start a process of constant healing that gradually intensifies the more you reshape and resolve your karmic patterns. Your vibrations will noticeably become more intense as you begin transcending over the earthly plane.

Meditation

Meditation is one of the foundations of spiritual preparation before accessing the Akashic Records. The first step is defining an intention. Using a laser-focused intention will keep you on to your mark throughout your whole journey through the Akashic Records. Since you're still starting out, try to simplify your intention to keep it direct and easily recognizable later on. You can choose something that happened in your childhood but is still bothering you, but it shouldn't be a traumatic or heavy experience. Set the unwinding and untangling of this event as your target as you enter the Akashic Records.

Once you're sure about the intention, start relaxing your body through deep breaths and closing your eyes. The second most important step is going into higher planes than the one you're currently existing in. Starting from your heart, slowly try to expand your sensations to engulf your surroundings. Your consciousness expansion can't be sudden; it should be gradual because you can easily get distracted if you don't move at a reasonable pace. Your consciousness has the potential to infinitely expand, and it's been doing it for quite some time now; before being born, during sleep, meditation, and death.

You'll begin to feel calmer, the more your consciousness expands. If you start doubting whether you've reached consciousness expansion or not, redo the process. If you suddenly feel like you see things from an outside perspective, it's the perfect opportunity to explore your Akashic Records. Begin to slowly unwind the event and recognize where responsibility lies. You'll notice that there is extra space to let in joy. Feel the happiness and rejoice amidst the vibrations of joy.

Chapter Six: How to Heal

Turbulence and times of distress go hand in hand with living. At one point in life, you will get to live an experience, no matter how big or small, that it is going to be a turning point. It will be like a wake-up call where you feel it is time to take the reins of your life and start to seek healing. Healing from abusive relationships, from traumas caused by losing a loved one, or perhaps from shock after miraculously surviving a fatal accident. In most cases, they are the monumental events that you witness in your life that force you to hit the pause button and realize it is time to actively try to get past them and move on with the life you always envisioned for yourself. However, in other cases, healing is not triggered by obvious transpiring. Instead, it can be a feeling of unsettling and lack of fulfillment from the life you are leading, so you decide to do something about it. As we discussed in previous chapters, accessing your Akashic Records can be of great help during your healing process. Uncovering key information about your past lives and what your soul has been up to will lead you to the root cause of some of the issues you are dealing with in your current life. Many people are at first drawn to the Akashic Records out of curiosity; however, they tend to continue this practice after they see first-hand how their healing journey has improved and come into fruition. In this chapter, we will talk about healing, what it means, how can you achieve it, and the role the Akashic Records play in this sought-after state of mind.

What is Healing?

The healing that we talk about here is not a physical one, but rather it is the kind of healing that takes place on a deeper subconscious level. It is the healing that fixes the metaphorical heartbreak and wounds of the soul. Although this spiritual healing depends on energies that you do not get to see, when you reach it, it will turn your whole life upside down. When you are healed, you will start to see the world through different eyes. You will learn how to deal with your pains and overcome future ordeals because you already have the tools you need to heal yourself, and you simply recall them. As we move forward, you will get to learn that acceptance and love are the cornerstones of healing. All experienced healers will tell you that unless you approach the Akashic Records with acceptance towards whatever you might find, you won't be able to reap the benefits of this powerful experience. The Universe operates in great precision with everything that happens, and these things happen for a reason. It is your responsibility to make sense of your life experiences, and that is exactly why you need to suffer in the first place and then go looking for ways to heal. It is believed that the Universe uses pain to grab your attention and let you know that you are straying away from your destined path. But just because the records are already there and you are expected to walk through a certain path, it does not mean that your pain is inescapable, and you are destined to endure it for eternity. As we explained in previous chapters, you are free to rewrite the story of your present life should you wish.

The Healing Aspect in the Akashic Records

Based on what we learned so far about the Akashic Records, your healing powers already exist within, all you need is some guidance to tap into these powers and put them to motion. When you go to an Akashic Records reading, the reader is simply using the records as a medium to invite the healing energy that exists within the Universe to come through. So, you can think of the Akashic Records as a tool used to enable you to reach healing. What is magical about this process is how your mind will quickly pick up on the healing information that it perceives during a reading. You will feel like you have been there before, and you know exactly what you should do. What happens during the readings is that you are unearthing capabilities and knowledge from your deep subconscious towards the shallower conscious, so you can utilize them in your present life. Learning that you used to be a queen in medieval times can be a good enough reason to convince you to change your self-demeaning ways, which are costing you a lot of pain and sabotaging your relationships. What is even more interesting is that the healing you seek through the Akashic Records can work the other way around. You might need to work on healing your previous selves so that they can reflect on your present one.

The records will shed light on burdens and heaviness that weighed you down in past lives and traveled through into your life today. In such cases, you will have to focus on working in the past so that you can give yourself the best chance to enjoy a fully healed future. The Akashic Records are more purposeful than you think, they will allow you to see what you need to heal the specific pains that you are suffering from at the time you reach out. Given how overwhelming the amount of data they hold, it would be useless to subject you to their immensity; instead, they are there to help you and walk with you while you do the work to heal. The idea is fascinating and stresses on the fact that when it comes to healing your soul, all you really need is "yourself" with all its complex layers manifested in different dimensions.

How to Heal

Now that we have reached the meat of this chapter, it is time to look at the different ways of healing that the Akashic Records can guide you through:

- Find Answers About Your Life

Among the millions of questions that run through your mind daily, there are more pressing ones that command your attention and are important enough to urge you to go look for answers. Such questions might be about your origins, who your ancestors were, and how everything is affecting your life. You could also be wondering about your love life and whether you should initiate a relationship with a certain person. The answers to these questions can only exist beyond our physical world. The Akashic Records can help you find what you are looking for; it is the only place where you can find information about your lineage and evidence of whether your potential suitor is your soul mate or not. This will give you the leverage you need to cure past traumas or cut ties with an unsuitable partner so you can reach contentment. Maybe you thought that you were bound to go through life blindly making monumental decisions that will impact all areas of your life. However, now you should know that you have the choice to call upon the powers of the Akashic Records and tip the scales in your favor.

- Clear the Mess

Like all people, you must be guilty of allowing negative feelings and energies into your life. Maybe you have been resorting to violence and inflicting pain on others as well as yourself without meaning to, or for reasons beyond your control. By looking through the Akashic Records, you can finally have the answers you need to identify the source of this behavior so that you can have a chance to fix it. Many people who suffer from similar behavioral disorders often find that abuse has been part of their past lives, and they have never come to terms with accepting it as a flaw that they must deal with. It is a unique opportunity to clear the mess that has been accumulating and replace it with more amiable qualities so that you can heal to be the person you know deep down you are.

- Unlock Your Potential

As we mentioned earlier, maybe your healing journey is not one of correcting wrongs, but instead, it is about accessing your full potential. Living a limiting life that does not honor the potential that you, as an individual, are uniquely blessed with can be your ailment. You will realize from the Akashic Records just how special you are and how many areas in your personality are yet to unfold. This powerful knowledge of your own capabilities will liberate you from the self-imposed prison that is boxing you into a less fulfilling life than the one you are entitled to. It is funny how sometimes we need some external medium to give us a clearer look and make more sense of what lies within the deepest corners of our beings.

- Befriend Your Soul

There is no chance of living in harmony unless your mind, body, and soul are aligned. Balance is the most powerful law that is governing our existence; when it is interrupted, you immediately feel that there is something wrong with your life. Your problem can be described as a simple imbalance. However, the same cannot be said about the magnitude of this turbulent relationship that you have with your soul. Through the Akashic Records, you will get to understand how compared to your soul, your body is an infant. Your soul, on the other hand, has been accumulating wisdom through its journey, so you need to seek amendments. Show your soul the respect it deserves and do not ignore it as a mere "voice from within," learn how to listen and benefit from its lessons. You will go through different situations where your mind has come to a certain decision, but your soul is not quite on board; this is exactly the time where you will feel the pain that you have to attend to. Do not fight your soul; learn to let it have its way so that you can move forward in your healing journey.

- Open Your Eyes to the Possibilities

Once you acknowledge the vastness of this Universe, and the endless possibilities that it has to offer, you will be less likely to accept defeat and will be inspired to heal and start anew. During Akashic Records Regressions, you can get to live through one of the many possible lives that you can potentially enjoy, or you had at some point. This transformative demo will compel you to see your present life as a blank canvas that you get to paint and repaint, however and whenever you wish. You will stop seeing yourself as a victim of the circumstances you are surrounded by and can choose to explore the myriad of possibilities that are waiting for you.

- Have Affirmation That You are On the Right Path

While the possibilities you have are infinite, your body, unfortunately, is not. Time is not on your side, so if you want to make sure you go as far as you can in your healing journey, you will need some affirming signs. This time, the Akashic Records can provide some signs to let you know if you are indeed on the right path. By pulling future records and opening a window into your future self, you will be able to make better decisions in the here and now. This comforting knowledge will be good enough for you to feel like you are doing your best and are trying to make sure that you are living up to what is expected of you.

- Cultivate Positive Energy

Energy is ever moving, and that constant state of flowing is always changing in nature and characteristics. You want to make sure that you always make way for positive energy to flow through your life. This is an important part of healing, knowing how to attract the right kind of energy when you need it the most. Given the elusive nature of energy, this can be one of the hardest parts of your journey. However, once again, the Akashic Records can lend you a helping hand by showing you exactly where energy tends to get trapped so that you can clear the blockage and help it travel through. When you learn how to access your records easier and faster, this mission, that seems impossible at first, will become much more obvious to you, so that you can pinpoint immediately where you need to get to work.

• Realize Your Strength

You cannot say that you are completely healed unless you have fully grasped your own strength. You will need this realization to lean upon whenever you want to undergo further healing. The Akashic Records will confirm that you can harness your strength as you did before and as you will continue to do well into the future. It is how your healing process can come full circle.

• Stop Patterns From Your Past Lives

If you remember, we have talked extensively about past lives in chapter 4 of this book, and how they affect the healing process. When the Akashic Records uncovers old and lingering patterns, you can have a clearer idea about your pain areas. It is important to note that learning how to master the skill of scanning through your past to make necessary healing changes will need some time, patience, and courage to dig through the old files.

• Feel Like You Belong

The connections you get to feel with the Universe and all creatures, human and otherwise in this life, is what accessing the Akashic Records will reveal to you. As a human being, you will always want to feel like you belong to something bigger, and this is a healing power. Knowing that you are not alone and that you have all the support that you might ever need can be an agent to recovery, and you will be able to heal completely.

Healing is an ongoing process; you do not get to do it once and think that it should last you a lifetime. It takes commitment and a lot of work to be able to create a healing practice that can work for you time after time. Every day you are living, there is potential pain waiting to disrupt your peace and take over your life. Unless you know how to deal with this pain, and how to approach it fully knowing that you already have all the tools you need to conquer it, you will be standing in your own way. If you are going to be attempting an Akashic Records reading, you should know that you must be well prepared for what you might learn. Many people go for it reluctantly, underestimating its powers, and end up being either disappointed thinking "it does not work for them," or they go into a state of shock after being overwhelmed by its intensity. In the next chapter, you will get to learn everything you need so that you can be prepared for accessing and reading your Akashic Records.

Chapter Seven: How to Access and Read Your Akashic Records

You might now be curious about how you can finally access and read the Akashic Records. The process of reading your own records and reading someone else's can be vastly different. However, this chapter focuses on reading your own records. Before you start using the Pathway Prayer to access the Records, you need to follow some simple rules to make sure that your readings go without a hitch.

Rules to Keep in Mind When Accessing the Akashic Records

Alcohol and Drugs Hinder You

Not only do alcohol and drugs distort your perception of reality, but they also affect your soul's vibrations and aura. When you are not fully in control of yourself, your energy field will be distorted. During any reading of the Akashic Records, the reader's aim should be uncovering the truth. Nonetheless, this cannot be achieved if your perception is not in its optimal state. Also, it is quite disrespectful to enter the Akashic realm in such a state. Remember, you will be in the presence of the Lords, Masters, Teachers, and Loved Ones.

Although they have only pure love for you, you should not take the gift they are giving you for granted. So, it is best to steer away from drugs and alcohol at least twenty-four hours before you attempt a reading. We, of course, are excluding prescription drugs from the rule. You need your prescription medicine to stay in tip-top shape, so it makes sense to continue taking it even if you want to attempt reading your records. Rest assured that any prescription medications should not have any impact on the quality of your experience in the Akashic realm.

Your Legal Name Matters

Names are powerful entities, and you should not underestimate the power your name possesses. All names have varying vibrations, and by using your legal name, your records will know that it is indeed you and allow you to seek knowledge from the Akashic realm. When trying to open your Akashic Records, you should always use your full legal name, not any variation that you go by daily. This means you should avoid using nicknames as well when opening the Records. Nevertheless, there are some exceptions to this rule. For instance, if you have recently gotten married and had to change your last name and take your husband's, you might still feel that your name does not truly reflect who you are. Because your new last name has not been fully integrated into your soul and identity, you might opt to use your original surname instead. Similarly, if you have recently contemplated getting a divorce or feel unsatisfied with your marriage, you may also use your maiden name without any consequences.

Immersion When Reading the Records Is Crucial

When you open the Akashic Records, your state of consciousness shifts as you go deeper than ever before. Therefore, you should spend enough time in the records to get to that state of consciousness. Take the time to observe what you can see, hear, or even smell. The Akashic realm offers a new exciting experience, so you should make the best out of it. Aim to stay around 15 minutes to a full hour in the Akashic realm to get a feel of it. Nothing is stopping you from spending more than an hour in the Akashic realm. However, your readings should not interfere with your productivity or life in general. The Records are there to guide you, not distract you. To prevent yourself from getting side-tracked, keep your sessions between 15 minutes and one hour for maximum benefits.

A Mix of Rituals Is Not the Best Approach

You might be already practicing other rituals; reading your records should not be affected if you do not mix rituals. Some rituals, for example, require that you ingest psychedelics or other drugs to take your perception to the next level. Yet, as mentioned in a previous point, drugs, alcohol, or any substance that alters your perception can be dangerous when you are trying to read the Akashic Records. While you are certainly free to pursue other rituals as well, it is always better not to mix them with a reading of your records, especially if their rules go against those of reading the Records. Even if their rules do not contradict with each other, keeping your reading sessions and other rituals separate always yields better results.

Some Questions Work Better than Others

When you are trying to access your records for the first time, it is easy to feel overwhelmed. Akashic Records offer a new realm of vast knowledge, so you might not know which questions to ask. Some forms of questions work better than others. Yes/no questions do not work well because the Lords, Master, Teachers, and Loved Ones do not give definitive answers, lest they sway your opinion. While you may want to ask those knowledgeable beings about what you should do, they will never give you a straight answer. If you ask a yes/no question, they will probably follow your question with even more questions! By doing this, they will take you on a journey of self-reflection through which you can find the answer on your own. In this sense, it is always better to ask questions that start with how, what, or why. Let's say that you are having doubts about your current romantic relationship and are not sure whether you and your partner are ready to get married. Instead of asking, "Should we get married?" you can say, "What will our marriage look like?" or "How will getting married affect our relationship?" Such forms of questions usually enable you to get better insights and helpful answers.

The Role of the Lords, Masters, Teachers, and Loved Ones

Throughout the book, the Lords, Masters, Teachers, and Loved Ones of the Akashic Records have been mentioned a few times. Although you might now be able to guess what they do, you still need to fully understand their roles before reading your records for the first time. Not only do they have different roles, but they have different natures too.

The Lords of the Records

The Lords of the Records is the highest authority in the Akashic Realm. They are the keepers of the Records and their protectors. They are entities made of light, and their sole goal is to enrich humanity and improve people's lives, helping them reach their divine ideal. Because they are responsible for keeping the Akashic Records safe, they have the power to either accept or reject people's entrance to the Akashic realm. However, the Lords do not do that to strip people of their right to read their own records but rather because they might not be ready to do so.

Reading the Akashic Records requires a huge deal of spiritual power and flexible thinking, which might not be feasible for everyone in the present moment. Moreover, when you ask a question, they can choose to withhold information if they think it is unwise to give you such information at that moment. The Lords do not reveal themselves to you, but they pass the information to the Masters, Teachers, and Loved Ones who, in turn, help guide you.

Everyone's Akashic Records are guarded by the Lords, which means that the Lords are not assigned to you specifically.

The Masters

The Masters are also beings made of light. As opposed to the Lords, every Master is assigned to a specific group, meaning that the Masters do not have a universal responsibility like the Lords, but they rather focus on individuals. Even if you have been reincarnated a dozen times, your Masters remain the same. For this reason, you may sense that they feel familiar when you are in their presence. Think of the Masters as your soul's keepers; they just want your soul to grow, gain more experience, and learn specific lessons. According to your needs, when you open the records, the Masters can call for the help of certain Teachers and Loved Ones who can help you with your endeavors.

The Teachers

Teachers are a bit different from the Masters or Lords when it comes to their prior history. It is usually claimed that they have been normal human beings in another life before they chose to help other souls reach their divine ideal. As elaborated on in the previous point, the Teachers are called upon by the Masters based on your needs. So, this means you can have different Teachers each time you open your records.

Teachers are lesson-specific, meaning that, once you learn a lesson, they will leave, and other Teachers will take their place to teach you a new lesson. The Teachers' identities when they were alive are a subject of debate, as some experts believe that they were ordinary people who just happened to have great spiritual power while others believe that they were influential figures. Regardless of these opposing opinions, the Teachers prefer to keep their identity a secret because they believe that this information is irrelevant to your soul's journey to growth.

The Loved Ones

The Loved Ones were certainly regular people once. Not only that, but they were also tied to you before their death. Your Loved Ones might be deceased relatives, friends, or even acquaintances. It does not matter how brief your relationship was when they were alive; you must know that your Loved Ones intentionally chose to guide your journey. Similarly, to how the Teachers act, the Loved Ones also think it is better not to uncover their true identities. However, they may do so if they think it can be beneficial during a specific reading. Your Loved Ones are not usually present all at once; they take turns to support you during every reading.

A Guide to How You Can Read Your Records

Understanding the Pathway Prayer and the role of the Lords, Masters, Teachers, and Loved Ones, it is finally the right time to access your records and take control of your destiny. Keep in mind that, given the right preparations, the process of reading your records should be easy. To make sure that you can access your records currently, follow the next few steps.

Finding the Right Place

As you advance, you will be able to access your records anywhere, anytime. Yet, for the purpose of this chapter, we are assuming that it is your first time opening the Akashic Records. Thus, this will require finding a quiet place where you can concentrate. It does not matter whether the place is indoors or outdoors if it offers you a sense of privacy. You can also burn some incense to set the mood and help yourself relax. If you have any pets or children, make sure that they cannot disturb you during your reading session. Moreover, you can play some classical music if you prefer not to stay in a completely quiet area.

Meditating

This step is crucial if you want to get an accurate Akashic reading. Meditating is a great way of centering and grounding yourself. When you enter the Akashic realm, you want to be free of your daily worries, and to achieve this; you need to keep your mind blank. For some people, it may prove hard to just pull the plug and relax. Nonetheless, by practicing meditation for a few minutes before each session, you can reach a state of inner nirvana that will help you communicate well with your Masters, Teachers, and Loved Ones.

Reading the Prayer

The Pathway Prayer creates a bridge through which you can reach the Akashic realm. When reading the opening prayer, try to read the first and last paragraphs out loud. When the Records are finally open, do not ask too many questions at once. As it is your first time to read the Akashic Records, you must get a feel of the Akashic realm, which means you should not ask any questions at first. Just try to take in as much as you can, then close the records after 15 minutes.

Focusing on a Question

After you get a feel of what the Akashic Records have to offer, you can reopen them after ten minutes or so. Now, it is the right time to ask your question. As explained previously, steer away from any yes/no questions and direct requests for advice. Also, you need to focus on one question at a time. Because you have past, present, and future records, you must decide which part of the eternal timeline you want to look at. Having this clarity is important if you want a seamless reading. Remember, your Akashic Records are always present, so do not worry if you cannot collect your thoughts now. You can just return to them later when you have more clarity on the questions you want to ask.

Grounding Yourself after Every Reading

Your consciousness shifts when you access the Akashic Records. You may think of it as a trance of some sort. Therefore, it is vital that you return to your normal state of consciousness when you close the Records. To come back to yourself and resume your day, you need to find an activity that requires your full attention—something that you cannot do mindlessly. You can do some stretches or exercises, cook, talk to a friend, or play with your pet. Under no circumstances should you skip this step. Grounding is an extremely important part of every reading session.

Practicing Your New Talent

Yes, accessing the Akashic Records is a talent. Everyone is born with the innate ability to access their records, but only those who practice enough can get a correct reading every time. For this reason, you need to open your Akashic Records as often as you can, especially during the first month. You can also practice your new ability by reading other people's records, which we will talk about in detail in the next chapter. In any case, do not ignore your Akashic Records for too long, as you need to get used to the shift of consciousness the process requires every time.

Keeping a Journal

Because you will learn many things during your time in the Akashic realm, you need to document your experience in detail. Keeping a journal is a great way of doing so. Not only will your journal allow you to describe your experience in that realm, but it will also help you keep track of all the feelings you may have. Furthermore, you can jot down the answers, future possibilities, and guidance you received during your readings. Also, feel free to write down any other questions that you want to ask during your next session. This will help you identify the past records that need to be rewritten, the current patterns you want to change, and the future possibilities that you want to either avoid or make use of.

Chapter Eight: Reading for Others

The Difference Between Reading Your Akashic Records and Reading Someone Else's

There are some core differences between opening and reading your own Akashic Records and helping someone else by reading their records for them. When reading for others, there are some guidelines that you must follow. Such guidelines are vastly different from the guidelines we have established in the previous chapter. Reading the records of another person is both an honor and a privilege, so you should be ready for this responsibility. Here are some of the guidelines you can follow to give a successful Akashic reading:

Consent Is Crucial

Akashic Records hold a person's every thought, emotion, action, and intent. They are the records of their life, and they also contain the records of the past ones. As you can infer, letting someone else read your records can make you feel vulnerable because you are trusting them with every detail of your life. Therefore, it is extremely important not to force reading on anyone. You need to get the person's explicit consent if you want to give them an Akashic reading. Also, do not try to manipulate them into giving you permission. In fact, it is even preferable that your clients or loved ones come to you asking for a reading, not the other way around.

As you gain more experience, you may be able to discern others' needs and find out that they indeed need a reading. Ultimately, it is not your choice. If the other person shows some hesitation, it means that the Lords of the Records do not think it is the right time for that person to know more. Regardless of the person's final decision, you need to continue providing love and support.

Discretion Is Key

This one goes without saying, but we need to make sure that you are aware of the secrecy any Akashic reading should involve. As mentioned previously, a person's records contain a depiction of their whole life. When you are chosen to help someone else know more about themselves, you become their secret keeper. For this reason, you must prove to that person that they had made the right choice when they trusted you by upholding a code of secrecy. This means that you should never divulge any information about the readings you give others, even if you are not disclosing strictly private details. Sometimes, you might want to tell people about your growing experience and how you are using your talent to help others. Yet, it is better to keep it to yourself unless the person agrees to share the details of their sessions. Put yourself in their shoes; would you like it if someone else shared your most private details with strangers?

Clarity Matters

People who give others Akashic readings often report that they do not fully understand the information or images they are presented with. Well, rest assured that this is completely normal. Because you are reading another person's records, not everything you are going to see or hear is going to make sense. Nonetheless, it is your duty to inform the other person of what you have seen. You'd be surprised that they might be able to make sense of it. In any case, it is crucial that you remain gentle, supportive, and respectful when presenting the information. Keep your readings free of judgment and make them a safe place for anyone who needs your help.

Minors Are Easily Influenced

You should never try to open a minor's Akashic Records because they are still being shaped. If you attempt to give a minor an Akashic reading, you risk influencing them and changing their future in some way, especially if you opt to open their future records. Moreover, this involves an even bigger moral dilemma—the issue of consent. Minors do not have the mental maturity required to consent; this is why any attempt to get their permission is considered coercion. So, what should you do if a minor's parents ask you to open his or her records? The short answer is that you should say no. Nevertheless, you can instead get their permission to access their own records if they have any questions about how they can improve their parenting methods. This way, you can still help the parents and respect the minor's rights at the same time.

Your Emotions Can Get Entangled

Objectivity is vital when you are giving someone else an Akashic reading. As you are going to be presented with intimate information about their lives, you must view this information and relay it objectively. Try to eliminate your own emotions from the equation to avoid upsetting the other person. You also should not give the person direct advice based on what you have seen in their records; you should allow them the freedom to choose how they are going to use the information you have given them. If you notice that you keep getting upset, or even angry, when people do not act on your advice, then you should take a break from giving others Akashic readings until you feel you can approach the sessions with impartiality.

What to Do If You Cannot Get a Person's Consent

You may find that you are either met with resistance or hesitation when asking others to open their Akashic Records. While this may signal that it is not the right time in most cases, the resistance or hesitation you might face can be easily remedied. If you cannot get a person's permission to read their records, there are two things you can do.

Reassuring Them

The easiest thing you can do is to alleviate any doubts the other person might be having. The person's resistance to letting you open their records could stem from some misconceptions they have about the Akashic Records, in general. They may think that they are not real or that accessing the Records will put them in unnecessary danger. You first must understand where the other person is coming from to help them get over their fears and doubts. In most cases, having a sincere talk about the nature and merits of opening the Akashic Records will convince the person to give you their permission.

Opening Your Own Records

If you have hit a dead end and cannot get the other person's permission no matter how hard you try to reassure them, then it is time to step back and respect their wishes. However, this should not stop you from continuing to give them your support in every way they need. Opening your own records is a great means of doing so. By opening your records and talking to your Masters, Teachers, and Loved Ones, you can ask them how you can help that person reach their divine ideal. Your Masters, Teachers, and Loved Ones will provide you with effective ways of helping the other person's soul grow and learn new lessons even if you cannot open their records now.

How to Conduct an Akashic Reading for another Person

After following the above guidelines and reassuring the person of the safety of opening their Akashic Records, you can now proceed to access and read their records. You need to use the Pathway Prayer Process mentioned in the third chapter. Nonetheless, the way you read the Prayer is going to be a bit different. Here is a breakdown of the full process:

Preparing Yourself

When you are trying to open someone else's records, you should always prepare yourself first. You need to let go of your worries, especially if you are usually plagued with thoughts of inadequacy. The core difference between reading your own records and reading another person's records is that you might suffer from stage fright when it is time to conduct a reading. To fix this, you must put the other person's needs first, meaning that you must focus on how the reading will benefit them instead of dwelling on your own emotions. You can meditate for a few minutes to alleviate stress and become ready to start the session.

Opening and Closing the Records

Because you want to put the other person at ease, the way you read the Pathway Prayer must reflect that. The first paragraph of the opening prayer should always be read out loud to signal your intention to open the Akashic Records. On the other hand, the second paragraph deals with the personal feelings of the reader - you – so it should not be read out loud. By reading the second paragraph, you actively call upon God to protect you from selfishness and help you stay focused on the reading. You should keep in mind that the third paragraph is where the biggest change lies.

Based on the previous chapters, you should now be aware of the importance of using the person's legal name when opening their records. Yet, because you do not want to make the person feel out of depth, you can use their first name or even nickname when reading the third paragraph out loud. Then, you can read the paragraph again by subvocalizing it, using the person's legal name. Finally, the last line should always be read aloud, as it signals that you have successfully opened the Akashic Records. While the opening prayer is different when giving another person reading, the closing prayer is the same. So, after you get the information you need, read all the lines of the closing prayer out loud to show your gratitude for the Masters, Teachers, and Loved Ones.

Grounding Yourself

Your consciousness shifts as you open the Akashic Records, then it shifts again to its normal state when you close them. You may notice that, after closing the person's records, you still feel some residual emotions from the reading. As you enter the person's records, you experience their past lives and troubles firsthand. Therefore, you could still feel a bit disoriented even after you close their records. Nevertheless, you have nothing to worry about. By finding an activity that requires your full attention, or what we call a grounding activity, you can let go of all the residue the reading session has left.

Things You Can Do to Ensure the Integrity of the Reading

Find Somewhere Quiet

Your goal as an Akashic reader should be finding the truth, and this requires a quiet area where you can stay focused. If you are conducting the reading in your house or office, make sure that the area is free of distractions and noises. On the other hand, if you are conducting the reading in the person's house, you must ask them to prepare a quiet area beforehand. If the Akashic Records are open, you have to make sure that nothing can distract you both. So, as you can see, every Akashic reading requires some serious preparations.

Be Careful When Giving Remote Readings

Not having the other person in the same room does not mean you cannot open their records. You can still conduct remote readings either online or on the phone. However, you must ensure that your technology is up to the task. You must make sure that your phone or laptop is fully charged. Also, you need to check your internet connection to avoid any connection issues during the session. According to what the person needs, they may ask you to record the session, so make sure that you have a functional camera around.

Get Finances Out of the Way

There is no shame in charging a fee for your readings. In fact, you might be able to turn your talents into a profession as you become more advanced and attuned to the energy of the Akashic realm. If you have already chosen to charge a fee, make sure to collect it before you start the reading, just to get it out of the way. This way, you can focus solely on accessing the other person's records and helping them reach their divine ideal. However, we do not recommend that you charge a fee directly after you open your own records for the first time. Because you need enough practice to be able to justify charging a fee for your readings, offer free readings for the first two or three months.

Have a Ready Set of Questions

Just like when you are reading your own records, you need to have specific questions in mind when reading the records of other people. Of course, you will not be able to come up with a list of questions you need to ask on the other person's behalf without discussing it with them first. Thus, you need to ask the person to prepare the questions they want to ask. In this spirit, you must elaborate on the difference between question forms and which ones work better than others.

If you still get a list full of yes/no questions, you can discuss with the other person how you can paraphrase such inquiries and change them into questions that start with why what, and how. Similarly, you need to let the other person know that they will not be able to ask personal questions about someone else unless they share a relationship with that individual. In any case, the information they will get about the other person will be limited to the context of their relationship.

Repeat the Pathway Prayer

Despite your best attempts, you may still feel like there is an invisible barrier between you and the person's records. Additionally, your emotions may become entangled in the reading, negatively impacting your impartiality. If this happens, you can read the Pathway Prayer again to get rid of any negative energy or tension you might be sensing. The Prayer's job is to clarify your aura and help you see the truth, so whenever in doubt, repeat the Prayer, and then continue where you left off.

The Benefits of Reading Others' Akashic Records

Gaining More Experience

The more time you spend in the Akashic realm, the more experience you gain, and the easier it becomes to shift your consciousness when needed. Not only will this enable you to help others reach their divine ideal, but it will also improve your own personal readings down the line. As time passes, accessing and reading your records will become easier. Not only that, but you will also be able to get an accurate reading every time. So, even if you do not get any monetary gain from it, reading other people's records can help you become more experienced with the Akashic realm.

Becoming More Attuned to Others' Needs

As you conduct more and more readings for others, you will notice that you are becoming more attuned to their needs. You will be able to relay the information you have been given as gently and respectfully as you can. Moreover, your perception will go beyond this physical realm, as you will be able to see other people in the light of the Akashic Records. This means you are going to be able to love all souls equally without any prejudice. Also, you will get rid of any judgmental patterns of behavior you might have had in the past and replace them with unequivocal love and acceptance.

Chapter Nine: Exercises and Meditations

Accessing your Akashic records will help you in keeping alignment with your real purpose. Once you connect with your soul and understand the reason behind your existence, it will be easier to find an avenue of escape from the worrisome, egotistic, fearful mind. Different meditation exercises are mostly designed to teach you the most beneficial questions you can ask to strengthen your connection with your Akashic records. This way, you will have a deeper connection, which will provide you with the guidance you are seeking. You can tailor these exercises to fit your life, experience, and desires. These meditation exercises can help you in all aspects of your life; personal, professional, and even with your romantic relationships. However, they are worthless if you can't open your mind and heart to the truth and guidance, they will help you unlock.

Exercise 1: Open Your Heart Center

This is the first exercise you must dip into in order to escape the mind that reverberates with fears, troubles, and doubts. Silencing your mind will enable you to be more open to all the information and power you will unlock by accessing your Akashic records. Beginners who aren't used to meditation or opening their heart centers can still master this technique with some simple steps, such as letting their muscles relax until they can no longer feel their bodies and start to feel their minds quieten. Be grateful for the progress you achieve until you reach a point where you are no longer distracted with a random train of thoughts and doubts. All you need to do is to be present now with comfort and ease while taking deep unhurried breaths.

1. Try to breathe in and out as calmly and slowly as possible. With each passing breath, try to let go of your worries and allow your thoughts to drift away.

2. Notice where your train of thought leads you without interrupting it or trying to force it to focus on any thought. Just be attentive to how each thought makes you feel while it's being lifted out of your head.

3. Close your eyes and take another deep breath. This time try to visualize your thoughts drifting away like a weightless cloud until they disappear into the void.

4. Take another deep breath and try to relax your face muscles as much as you can. Make sure that your shoulders and back aren't rigid. Try to let go of any tension in your mind and body by simply breathing deeply in and out.

5. While you are relaxing even more, try to gently let your mind drift down into the center of your heart. Let your mind float peacefully into your heart center where tranquility and serenity emanate. At this point, you should start to feel a sense of divine love vibrating deep within your heart.

6. Allow the spark of divine love to slowly turn into a flame that ignites every part of your body and soul.

7. Immerse your body in the peace and light that radiates within your heart, filling you up.

8. You should feel a sense of familiarity and comfort that radiates from your heart center throughout your whole body until you start feeling connected to your eternal spirit that is open to receiving guidance and inspiration.

9. Whenever you are in a state of agitation, or if you need the calming experience, resort to the peace within. This is your eternal source of tranquility that never ceases to exist.

Exercise 2: Clearing Records of Time

To be able to clear the records of time and space, it's important to identify the times of your life where you often felt challenged. You need to be aware of the pattern of all the days, weeks, seasons, events, or even years that you feel brought you the most challenges that you can't seem to get over. You can seek the help of your Record-Journal to write down these events in clear notes to connect the dots to reach a clear pattern you can work with.

1. Start with the behaviors, thoughts, and emotions you felt at those times. Make sure to list all the tough ones you are trying to get rid of and clear out of your records.

2. At the same time, start listing all the empowering and pleasant thoughts and emotions you would like to replace your negative energies with.

3. After you have identified a clear temporal pattern of all the negative emotions you want to clear, visualize a clock with all the time periods you have in mind. This is when you might start noticing a lot of images or writings of the events you are trying to erase, unfolding before your eyes.

4. Without hesitation, see yourself wiping out all these images, thoughts, and writings until your clock is as clear as crystal.

5. Make sure to pay close attention to the words that will start to appear in your mind. Concentrate on erasing all negative words that might penetrate your thoughts. Then, try reinforcing positive emotions and energies, such as pleasure, relaxation, fulfillment, happiness, and blissful achievements. Visualize your clock with colorful hues and joyous images of yourself while you are experiencing your life in the way you desire.

6. After you have filled your clock with the happy moments you aspire to, it's time to rewrite all the dreadful past experiences you would like to change. Write down in your Record-Journal all the hardships you have gone through and the emotions they evoke within your heart.

7. Write down how you would like to approach these hard times and the different beliefs and attitudes you think would help.

8. Be kind to yourself while you remember all your mistakes. Implement self-empowerment, positive self-evaluation, and peace of mind. Move forward from self-loathing and all the cruel thoughts you have constantly criticized yourself with.

9. After you have drawn a clear path of all the experiences you want to rewrite and the different approaches you would like to take, begin to meditate with slow deep breaths.

10. Visualize a clear image of the place where you consistently go through these bad experiences. Envision yourself erasing all the dark shadows that roam in it with the affirmation in mind that you are letting go of all and any toxic attachment you might have once held towards that place.

11. "I am free and comfortable, I have a history, but I'm not my history." Repeat these words in your mind or even out loud while you imagine the place in question.

12. After you start feeling a wave of tranquility soothing your body, begin to visualize a more vibrant and happier version of the place, ignited by a beautiful warm light that is clearing all the darkness that once lived there.

When Your Purpose Piles Up

Each passing lifetime brings us different experiences through which we are directed to our purpose. Exploring these experiences and satisfying our purposes are our only gateways to emotional growth and, consequently, the evolution of our souls. These experiences slowly form a map to our soul to guide us forward in life. With passing time, we become more complex in terms of our minds, emotions, and reactions. It becomes harder to understand our feelings, motivations, and even our true selves. Therefore, you find so many people suffering from distorted self-images that push them to doubt their own perception of reality.

A critical part of record investigation is understanding the complex layers to ourselves. To heal and move forward, we must peel back these layers. This will not only help us in understanding our purposes, but it will also guide us to grasp a clear idea of who we really are. This journey of exploring one's soul truth will eventually give them the long-awaited healing for past and present pains.

When a certain unhealthy situation, emotion, or reaction persists, then it should give us a clear sign to start looking into the past to be able to understand the present. In these situations, looking into the causes and reasons why your karma is insisting on coming back is the only smart move. Only then can we begin to grasp the right way of looking into our souls to break free of these negative cycles. While some patterns are harder to unfold, you can still change your past, present, or even your future with a simple act. Once you manage to do the powerful shift of power and energy, you will be able to start getting rid of more problems and negative emotions with each step of this illuminating journey. Being less burdened with the difficulties we had in our past will allow us to be more open to the changes our future is holding, to become empowered and liberated.

Exercise: Unfold the Past

After you have understood the power held by unfolding the layers of complex reactions and emotions to understand our true selves, you need to start pinning down where it all seems to go wrong. This exercise might be taxing, but it is necessary for healing and being able to move forward.

1. Close your eyes and take deep long breaths.

2. Let your mind wander to the moments in your life where you felt frustrated, sad, and agitated without understanding the reason behind your misery. After accessing your records and unfolding the different layers to your emotions, most people find that there is one evil root behind all their misery. This is when the puzzle pieces should start coming together.

3. In your head, create a map of all the different difficult events and your reaction to them. Pay close attention to the repeated hard times. Do you get the feeling that there is a certain energy that is blocking your path to happiness? Do you get the feeling that there is a certain event that you are compensating for? Paying its price?

4. Determine what the obstacles are that are standing between you and your happiness, wealth, finding true love, the creativity you long for, and even the healing you desperately need.

5. Start identifying the pattern that is forming in front of your own eyes.

6. With each deep inhale and exhale, allow yourself to move from these hard moments.

7. Right here is when you should focus all your attention on relaxing your body and emptying your mind.

8. Looking into the records of the past, present, and future is easy when you understand that all time is happening and vibrating at the same time.

9. Focus all your attention on opening the source of every trouble you have gone through, each negative feeling you have experienced, and every evil thought that has made its way to your mind.

10. You will come to notice that there is a certain event that your mind seems to circulate back to despite your effort to move on from it.

11. Once you have defined that certain event you can't seem to ignore, let your mind explore it further, unfolding each aspect to it.

Exercise: Viewing Past-life Records

This exercise is designed to help you access the Sacred Temple and your Akashic Record Screen to witness an event from your past life. This isn't about just any random experience that already happened in your past life. It should be connected with your focused intention. Make sure to attentively follow the script after you have prepared your mind, heart, and soul to be open to any type of information on your Screen from your Akashic Records guide. This is a meditation process that encompasses two different phases, rather than just a one-time exercise. You can revisit this exercise whenever needed to tackle the same experience more than once, or different experiences that you would like to explore further before you begin with the second part of this experience that involves rewriting and changing what needs to be altered. You can use this technique to heal all sorts of traumas, emotional scars, and negative energies in your records.

- Just like any meditation exercise, start by putting your body and mind into a state of relaxation. Begin to count from six down to one. With each descending number, remember to take a deep breath as you begin to feel yourself diving deeper and deeper into a state of tranquility. Without forcing yourself, let your mind float gently to your Sacred Temple, where you usually find great comfort and peace while feeling deeply connected with your soul.
- Think of your Sacred Temple as a pool that you slowly dip your body into with each passing number you count. With each breath you inhale, focus on a certain part of your body. With each exhalation, focus on relaxing these body part muscles.
- Six: Relax your face muscles, letting go of any tension, especially in the forehead and eyebrows area.
- Five: Focus on loosening the muscles of your tense shoulders.
- Four: Feel your deep breaths filling up your abdomen area like an inflated balloon. Then exhale slowly to feel your stomach slowly going back to its original state, just like deflating a balloon gradually.

• Three: Let go of any tension in your lower body, appreciating all the times your legs have supported your weight.

• Two: As your body begins to dive deeper into relaxation, try to let go of all your concerns, worries, and fears. Let your mind drop into your heart center to be able to feel calmer and more relaxed.

• One: As you feel your body and mind slowly floating in your sacred temple, ride this warm wave of relaxation to get glimpses of your past life to be able to heal your current life.

Rewrite Past-life Experiences

This is the part of the same meditation process where you can utilize the information you have collected from the first part to break the negative cycle and release any energy you would like to let go of. This part would depend on rewriting the records of any event and its results, even if they were experienced for long periods during your past life. During this part, you should focus on giving yourself a new explanation or a different approach, one which can empower you in those situations to change the feelings of powerlessness and helplessness you felt in the past.

• Get to your favorite location where you can find the peace and quiet you need in this journey.

• Start your meditation session by relaxing your body and mind to have direct access to viewing the screen you have already unfolded from the previous exercise.

• Count again from six down to one until your body enters the same state just like before.

• This time, you have the chance to unfold the event in question differently. Instead of unfolding the layers of a traumatizing experience that leaves you weak and shaking, you can approach it proactively to have the upper hand.

• Instead of revisiting the event with doubt and fear, embark into the experience with confidence filling up your vessel to have the power to change what you need in order to rewrite your own past, present, and future.

Bonus 1: Eleven Powerful Akashic Prayers to Transform Your Life

You don't have to necessarily say Akashic prayer to be able to reap the healing and transformative benefits of Akashic records. But, when you're still starting your journey, prayers can do wonders for your body and soul, giving you profound results that can take years to get with other types of meditation. The Akashic prayers and exercises mentioned in this chapter are taken from both ancient and modern Akashic sources.

1. The Prayer of Permission

"As I stand in the light produced by this divinity, I'm humbly offering my body as a vessel for energy to flow within and through me. Please accept my request to access the Akashic Records."

This prayer is used daily before attempting to access your Akashic Records. While it may not be required, it's quite useful because you begin to humble yourself and lose your ego to be able to see clearly. Remember that your Akashic Records contain an infinite amount of information and energy; it's advisable to prepare your mind and soul to stay focused and avoid becoming overwhelmed.

The permission you're asking for isn't exactly directed to an outside external force. You're only trying to communicate to the divine that's already within you. You may be unaware of such divinity at first, but as time progresses, you'll begin to feel its presence inside you as you access the Akashic Records.

2. The Prayer of Alignment

"Source, universe, soul, spirit, and the divine, please hear me as I request to be guided through the brightest and highest of vibrations. Let me understand what the truth truly means. Whatever I receive, let it be my greatest aid in this life."

It's important to align your goals as you go through the Akashic Records. You need to ask yourself multiple questions about true intentions and reasons for the journey. This prayer will also remind you that you are a being that can transcend the worldly webs of illusions.

The directions you are asking for do not mean that you won't be able to find the way yourself once you're in the Akashic Records. They are like a totem that you keep looking at through your journey to remember what made you come here in the first place. The prayer will help you avoid getting trapped in loops and illusions created in the past, in addition to centering your direction throughout the journey.

3. The Prayer of Going Forward

"Mother, Father, Gods, Ancestors, Ancient Ones, help me sever the bonds of past lives. Let my wounds heal with time. Give me the courage to release this entrapped energy within me and let the light into my soul. I will replenish my old stagnant energy with overflowing energy. Let the river of light pass through every crevice of my soul."

This prayer will allow you to borrow from the energies of your family and the divine beings that surround the space around you. Your soul can absorb different forms of energy from multiple sources. Use it to your advantage while you're in the Akashic Records. While the energies around you are infinite, the odds of using all of it are slim. Borrowing from the divine beings inside and outside will help you synchronize the flow of energies through your soul.

4. The Prayer of Responsibility

"I no longer follow the paths that allow me to forfeit responsibility. I thereby choose not to blame anyone else for whatever that ails me, in the future, past, and present. I am the creator of my own human experience. I control the power to create my own divine experience, and I will never shift this responsibility to someone or something else."

One of the main problems that we face as we try to resolve our deepest issues is shifting the blame for what we go through. And this will never help you move forward. What's happened has happened, and there is absolutely no need for you to relive it and think about it, consuming your energy. Take responsibility not for hurting yourself but as acceptance for what you're feeling. Whatever happened in your past is probably something you're not responsible for, but it's your responsibility to change how you react to it.

5. The Prayer of Expulsion

"God, Goddess, Mother, Ancient Ones, I need your help to cleanse myself of energies that do not belong to me. My body, aura, and energy field are filled with energies, and I know that they carry no benefit to me. Help me release this energy and send it to the divine field, where they could be put to better use. Let me fill my spirit and body with the most personal and divine energies."

Carrying the energy of others without knowing can place a big burden on you. Piling up of energies inside your soul will keep you from being able to achieve higher frequencies of vibrations. This doesn't mean that impersonal types of energy will negatively affect you. On the contrary, some energies can be transferred from other people to aid you in your journey in the Akashic Records.

The type of energies you carry can belong to people who died thousands of years ago. Soldiers, kings, maids, children, and many other people who are connected to you through karmic patterns can leave a life-long imprint on your energy. It's up to you to release and expel these energies to get a new opportunity to create your own complete and perfect form of energy.

6. The Prayer of Energy Patterns

"I humbly call upon the powers of Archangel Michael and the Akashic Divinities of the Realms. It's only with your help that I can untangle the webs of shadows that elude my understanding. Help me clear the interferences of karmic patterns that surround my thoughts and vibrations. Cleanse the energies brought upon infinite dimensions through infinite planes. Allow me to mold my own karmic patterns through higher vibrations. Let those energies flow away into the infinite space, forever."

This prayer is more of an expulsion type of prayer rather than protection. The energies that negatively interfere with the Akashic process can sometimes be too strong to expel. Remember, the mass of this energy can be insurmountable, which is why you may need to call upon the power of high divine beings. Their generosity is simply astounding. Once you recite this prayer, you'll immediately notice how the low negative vibrations are escaping from your body.

Karmic energy patterns are known to be troublesome because of their ancient powers. While you may be able to reshape those patterns according to what you want to attract, it will probably take some time if you choose not to ask for help. This prayer is recommended for beginners because karmic patterns are best approached with extreme focus. The Akashic Records can and will show you how energy patterns can interfere with your soul's path. But changing those patterns to something else will be up to you.

7. Prayer of Ancestral Influence

"Hear me, please, Akashic beings of the divine. It's your help that I need to break the chains that have enslaved my soul for hundreds of years. Let me rejoice in the new light, unrestricted by chains that have been passed down to my soul. My body aches as it absorbs multitudes of awareness that weigh more than it can handle. Let my consciousness absorb all my ancestral heritage, and let it be aware of past and future generations. Let only the negative bonds be broken and leave nothing but the energy of oneness with the divine."

The ancestral family influence flows very deep through every soul on earth. It's impossible to reject all the energy brought through a bond that spans eternity. But it's still possible to reject and expel energies that do your soul harm. This prayer will help you take control of the energies that you draw from your ancestral origins. Every soul is different, but you'll find good and bad ancestry links within every single soul.

This task isn't an easy one, which is why you'll be using the powers of the Akashic beings of light. They are ancient forces that control the flow and mass of energy though infinite plateaus of the spiritual world. They will help you notice where your points of ancestral vulnerability lie. Unshackling yourself from the negative bonds of ancestors will make you feel light and able to create new spiritual memories for yourself.

8. The Prayer of Heaven

"As the power of the divine flows through me, I know I can create with grace whatever my heart desires. I will manifest the powers of creation to let my deepest desires of heaven on earth come to existence. My purpose is to become one with the universe, and to ultimately flow as energy through its endless creations."

One of the strongest powers of the Akashic Records is its ability to manifest "heaven on earth." Concentrating energies of endless magnitudes allows the divine being to create and attract what truly resides in the deepest parts of their soul. The Akashic aligning of energies allows you to compel the low-vibrating energies to change their vibrations according to your will. The type of energy you can emanate through this prayer will help you affect your external surroundings.

9. The Prayer of the Unknown

"Father, Mother, God, Divine One, Ancient Beings, let me know what I need to know to stay safe. If it's not possible, then please let me release the energy associated with my fear of the unknown. I will finally move free of worries and doubts as I relinquish my fear of the unknown."

One of the worst restrictors of humans is their fear of the unknown. By nature, humans are usually unaware of the effect of the energies that the future carries for them. This fear of the unknown can hinder your progress and stop you from reaching your goals because you'll be paralyzed by fear. When you're in a disturbed state, use this prayer as you enter the Akashic Records because it will help you stabilize the low vibrations.

10. The Prayer of Joy

"Divine beings of light, please let me see the pleasures of this world in their truest and purest form. Remind me how to enjoy the simple acts that I once used to rejoice in doing. Let the rays of the sun softly tickle my skin, and the wind to gently blow my hair again."

If there is one thing you should be looking for in the Akashic Records, it's your own happiness and that of those around you. Fortunately, accessing the Akashic Records reduces a lot of the stressors you have, removing a huge burden that can keep you from being happy and joyful. Many people think that achieving happiness is a task like the one given to Sisyphus, where a boulder must be pushed for eternity, falling down every time it reaches the top. But in fact, achieving happiness is much simpler.

Accessing the Akashic Records through this prayer will remove the cynicism and pessimism people have as they feel emotionally down. They'll understand that there is no such thing as a permanent state of energy, and it can be constantly modeled and reshaped according to an individual's will. Do not fall prey to the belief of not being in control of your conditions. Try to take responsibility for making yourself feel happy as long as you breathe. Yes, you may not permanently stay happy, but at least you'll be able to stay at a very close baseline.

11. The Prayer of Healing

"Mother, Father, God, Goddess, Ancient Ones, Divine beings of light, please hold my spirit as I try to heal the damage that has been done unto my soul. Let me receive the clearing energy on multiple dimensions and allow me to use all the energy you've given to me to fix what has been broken. Let the light find its way into the ancient and current wounds and drive it from within to restore my soul and body into its most perfect state."

This prayer can be used daily, and it's especially important if you feel that you're down and unable to resolve the problems that plague your day. It will allow you to borrow the power of divine beings that can help guide the energy through what ails you. Whether it's an emotional or a physical wound, you will still be able to heal it quickly if you let the Akashic Records restore the vibration to its original and perfect state.

Bonus 2: Introduction and Guide to Akashic Tarot Reading

Despite their vast importance as a critical map to our souls, Tarot started out as a simple parlor game for entertainment. The origin of tarot cards, as we know them today, goes way back to the 14th century. Artists in Europe created the first deck without the intention of creating a divinatory tool, but accidentally created one of the mightiest ones. These were simply intended as only an entertaining card game. The association between these cards and divination only started to appear in the 16th century or early in the 17th century. However, their use was of a much simpler nature than it is now.

Over centuries, specifically during the beginning of the 18th century, tarot managed to establish its significance as one of the most important tools of divination. Suggestions started to be made for the possible meaning each card might hold, laying out their divinatory purposes. Nowadays, the magic of these cards has drawn more and more people to finally establish tarot as the most popular among different types of psychic readings.

A Basic Overview

People aren't only drawn to Tarot just for their ease of use; they aren't as easy as reading tea leaves or other methods such as pendulums. Their gravity lies in the power they hold in understanding our higher selves and having a dependable gateway for interpreting what the future might hold for us. If you are still unfamiliar with the concept of divination and its different tools, you might fall under the wrong impression that tarot readings are equivocal to reading into the future. However, the truth is, while tarot cards are the closest thing we have to time machines, they still can't be used as a fortune-telling method by anyone and everyone. Bear in mind that grasping the concept and going through the guidelines of tarot is easy with practice, yet doing accurate readings isn't simple work; not everyone is cut out for this talent.

The Akashic Tarot

What started out as a simple deck of playing cards grew into hundreds and thousands of different options to choose from. You can find decks of cards that are based upon famous artwork such as movies, series, books, and more. However, there is one deck that has stood the test of time, and that is the Akashic Tarot deck.

This is one of the most significant and mighty decks available. The gravity it holds lies in the fact that this is the only deck designed for accessing the Akashic Records and unlocking their profound energy and abundant source of information. This tool is one of the most powerful ones that offer clear access to the higher mystical and magic powers that Akashic Records encompass. You can use this deck for tapping into great fields of wisdom and seeking guidance throughout different aspects of your life.

Maintaining Your Cards

The most important thing you need to look out for is protecting your tarot cards against any physical damage and keeping them clean from negative and evil energies. There are a few ways that you can do this, from consecrating your deck, wrapping the cards in a silk scarf, protecting them in a small box, or putting them in a cloth bag that is protected by a drawstring. Some people prefer to resort to a combination of these different methods to save them from any harm that could reach them.

How to Consecrate Your Magic Tools?

In Ancient Wicca and modern Pagan traditions, all magical tools should be consecrated before any attempts of using them to interact with the Divine. This ritual can still be used after you have already felt and played with your deck to expel any negative energy that might wrap your cards. This method comes in particularly handy in situations where you are not sure about the history of your magical tools, in terms of their past owners or who used them before they reached your path. However, you should bear in mind that some specific tools don't require any consecration before their use. Some practitioners view consecration as an unnecessary ritual that might disrupt their natural energy flow and confuse conscious and unconscious energy directions. Before cleansing their cards, some people prefer to get to know the deck by touching and feeling it.

Keep in mind that there is no right or wrong way of doing any ritual or even one solid purpose in doing it. Some people prefer to consecrate their magical tools and their jewelry, clothing, and the altar itself. The items used for this ritual are rather simple; you will need a white candle, a cup of water, incense, and a bowl of salt. Each item represents an element and direction to summon the powers of the North, South, East, and West with guardians of Air, Fire, Earth, and Water. Cast your circle if you need to to complete the ritual and cleanse your tools from any past owners or dark energy.

Akashic Tarot Cards as Gifts

There are three different beliefs when it comes to receiving a tarot deck as a present.

Some fortune-tellers believe that tarot decks lose their magnificence and spiritual values when they are received from someone else. These readers have strict rules against accepting tarot cards as a gift. However, there is one exception to this rule. If there is a person you trust, who is gifting them to you as a purely heartfelt gesture, then there isn't a strong reason that pushes you to return the gift. They can then be used after a good cleansing and consecration.

Some readers have a strong belief that tarot cards should never be bought. They must be received as gifts from people whom they have strong connections with, for the magic powers of love.

Some other readers don't really care about the source of their decks, regardless of whether they buy their own or receive them as gifts. The source doesn't make one bit of a difference as long as the cards are clean from any negative energies, and they don't have a wrong feel to them. What's important is the connection you build with your deck and the accuracy of your readings, rather than their source.

An Overview of Akashic Tarot Reading

Methods of reading have changed and evolved over the years. Since reading tarot cards is a highly intuitive process, many readers even adopted and developed their own unique ways of reading Akashic tarot cards. They played with the traditional meanings of the card layouts. However, we can't point out a significant change that fell upon the cards themselves. There are different guidelines, books, and charts that will come in handy for beginners who are still trying to figure out the basics of doing a reading. Yet, it's highly believed that the best way to the evolution of your talent is to start by feeling the cards, holding them, and trying to understand what they are telling you. However, some basic tips should be considered to get to know your cards and protect them before we begin to unfold the different aspects of learning how to do Akashic tarot reading.

If you are trying to get familiar with a brand-new deck of Akashic tarot cards, then the best way to get to know the deck is by placing them under the pillow you sleep on. This way, the cards will acquire your personal energy.

Never leave your cards scattered all over the place. If you are carrying the cards with you, you can't just leave them in your pocket or purse. Hold them in a protective shield until you reach your destination.

Many readers don't allow anyone else to touch their cards, to prevent the cards from absorbing any vibrations other than their own. Others might prefer for a reader to shuffle or cut the cards before they begin reading.

After cleansing your cards by consecrating them, you can limit their contact with any energies by storing them with a quartz crystal that absorbs all these energies.

If your cards have been handled by anyone and you don't feel comfortable with their presence, it's better to re-consecrate your cards or leave them until they feel right to you again.

These cleansing rituals aren't necessary if you don't feel the need for them. However, if you must do them or any other spiritual cleansing ritual, then it's important to do what feels right. Once you are comfortable with how your cards feel, you will notice how your readings will start to improve.

Guide to Akashic Tarot Reading

Just like any tool of divination, there is no wrong or right way of using it. Reading Akashic tarot cards is an intuition that could easily differ from one person to another. The focal point is to use the card in your own unique way that allows you to shape your psychic abilities. There are a different number of layouts and spreads that could be altered and switched between to achieve the highest accuracy of your reading session. The steps to reading Akashic tarot decks to unlock your higher self and open a window to the future should start by understanding your cards.

1. Get Ready for Your Reading by Interpreting the Cards

The deck is divided into two main groups, Major Arcana and Minor Arcana. To understand the basics of a traditional deck, we will go through the three parts of major Arcana that consists of 22 cards, or trumps. Before we dive deeper into the meaning behind each one of these cards, we need to quickly go through the Minor Arcana cards in the Akashic tarot decks that repaint the events of our daily lives. Each group represents an element of the four essential elements.

* Wands that represent Fire

1. Ace of Wands
2. Two of Wands
3. Three of Wands
4. Four of Wands
5. Five of Wands
6. Six of Wands
7. Seven of Wands
8. Eight of Wands
9. Nine of Wands
10. Ten of Wands
11. Page of Wands
12. Knight of Wands
13. Queen of Wands
14. King of Wands

* Pentacles that represent the Earth

1. Ace of Pentacles
2. Two of Pentacles
3. Three of Pentacles
4. Four of Pentacles
5. Five of Pentacles
6. Six of Pentacles
7. Seven of Pentacles
8. Eight of Pentacles
9. Nine of Pentacles

10. Ten of Pentacles
11. Page of Pentacles
12. Knight of Pentacles
13. Queen of Pentacles
14. King of Pentacles

* Also, there are Swords that represent Air, from the Ace of Swords up to the King of Swords, and Cups that represent Water, from the Ace of Cups up to the King of Cups.

The Major Arcana

* The First Part: The Material World (Cards 0-7)

The first part repaints the material world regarding job success, education, finances, and marriage.

0. The Fool: Despite what you might think, the fool is the wisest trump of the Major Arcana, the one who knows everything. It represents wisdom, enlightenment, and guidance. The fool symbolizes the eternal spirit of the deck painted with the soul of the inner child, trust, and innocence. It gives way to a new sense, a new cycle, or a new chapter in life.

1. The Magician: This card is the representation of the planet Mercury, with an infinity symbol over the head of the magician. It symbolizes a great mastering and control over all your conscious and unconscious processes.

2. The High Priestess: This is the card that represents emotions in Akashic tarot with its symbolization of intuition, the dream world, psychic energy, and all the feelings and instincts. She is a receptive mirror of the underworld and everything happening below the surface. This card related to the women's cycle in terms of fertility, the womb, and the magic that women hold.

3. The Empress: This card connects with the planet Venus. She is the goddess of love and the great mother of the tarot cards. This card relates to beauty, relationships, and peacemaking and has an artistic side. She indicates mothership and your relationship with other women in your life.

4. The Emperor: This tarot card comes with power, authority, leadership, responsibility, and action. Another side to him is masculine creativity, passion, and new beginnings. He is the father, leader, husband, authority figure, or the man in your life.

5. The Hierophant: This card symbolizes your connection with your God, guardian angel, and your higher self. This is a representation of practical wisdom and energy.

6. The Lovers: This is the favored card for almost anyone who enjoys tarot readings. It indicates a golden key to a variety of choices and relationships. The Lovers card represents Heaven, Earth, union, love, communication, duality, and the balance between the masculine and feminine energies we all hold within us.

7. The Chariot: This is the card that combines the emotional side with the body. It's a clear representation of controlling emotions, the need for emotional protection, family, caring, and nourishment.

2. Pick A Single Card

Before beginning this exercise, take the time to understand the meanings and different symbols that the cards hold. You also need to pay attention to the reversed meanings of the cards when they come up backward or upside down. Some readers believe that when cards are reversed, that simply means that their meanings are also reversed. For example, the Lovers card would represent hatred, insecurity, and isolation as opposed to its normal symbols.

This exercise is rather simple. All you need to do is to draw a card out of the first part of the Major Arcana randomly every day. As the day passes by, take some notes of its major events and how they relate to the card you drew from the deck early in the morning. Some fortune-tellers prefer to dedicate a notebook or keep a journal for every card they draw, with highlights of their days relating to each card. You can then look back at the end of every week to reflect on the card that appeared the most and which cards were drawn more than others. This exercise allows a much easier understanding of the main energy of your records and the experiences that paint your aura.

* The Second Part: The intuitive Mind (Cards 8-14)

While the first part of the Major Arcana focused on our interactions with the outer world regarding our family, friendships, love, and the emotions and instincts involved in different relationships, the second part is more about individualism. The cards in this group focus more on our individual beings rather than dealing with societal issues. This part deals with the intuitive mind using these seven cards that reflect how we feel more than symbolizing our thoughts. They are attuned to what our hearts need and our unending search for the truth and faith.

8. Strength
9. The Hermit
10. Wheel of Fortune
11. Justice
12. The Hanged Man
13. Death
14. Temperance

3. A Three Card Layout

After you have kept a habit of drawing a single card and documenting daily events that relate to these cards, you will have noticed a certain pattern or some regular trends that have announced themselves regularly over this period of time. Since you probably have gotten used to two-thirds of the Major Arcana, as well as the wands and pentacles of the minor Arcana, you should now be developing a sense of every card and its meaning and symbol.

Now, it's time to add the second part of the Major Arcana to the equation. Add to your pile all the wands and pentacles from Ace to King. Just like the previous exercise, shuffle your cards and make a habit of drawing, this time, three cards each morning rather than just a single card. Don't look at the cards you pull up as individuals, but rather as a whole. Pay attention to the way they fit together and how they are connected. Are all of them connected, or is there a certain card that seems to stand out every time? The rest of the exercise is the same as before, where you notice your daily events and how they relate to the cards you draw out every morning. You can continue the habit of keeping a journal of every pile you pull and all the highlighted events of your day.

* The Third and Last Part: The intuitive Mind (Cards 15-21)

You have already become familiar with the cards that deal with the material world and your connection to others, and you have added the second part that focuses on dealing with the intuitive mind and your individual being. The last part that encompasses the cards from the 15th and until the last card in the Major Arcana gives you a window to understanding universal laws and issues. This part is important as it deals with circumstances that might hold great importance in forming our present and future.

15. The Devil
16. The Tower
17. The Star
18. The Moon
19. The Sun
20. The Judgement
21. The World

* The last exercise is to draw a pile of five cards from the whole tarot deck, including both major and minor Arcana.

4. Akashic Records Using Tarot Cards

By now, you will have formed a connection with the cards, felt them, and investigated their deeper meanings. You can now use them to have easier access to your Akashic Records, to connect with your higher self. Once you master Akashic tarot readings, you will be able to open yourself to the guidance and wisdom your Akashic Records hold for you. Only then will you be able to read more into your future.

Conclusion

It's not easy to carefully balance the spiritual and worldly desires, especially if you are engulfed in personal wars that involve both spiritual and material elements. It's easy to see whether someone is living in harmony and tranquility or in instability caused by the many contradictions they have to accept to go forward. The link between the spiritual and material worlds is in the Akashic Records, transcending time and space, dealing with vibrations and energy. Your eyes may be able to carefully observe the present, but it's the Akashic Records that allow you to see beyond the present and into the past and future.

The material provided here shall be your ammunition as you grapple between the different and contrasting worlds of your life. Use the Akashic Records to integrate the domain of the spiritual world into the material one. You can rest assured that the happiness and joy you'll attract will be infectious, as you'll be sensing not only your energy but also others'. The wisdom you'll gain through accessing the divine will show you the true direction of your soul, which is to embark on a journey of honesty, truth, and goodness.

Finishing this book means that you are truly invested in bettering your inner soul. Never lose this momentum as time goes by, and make sure to always invest in it, attracting what you truly desire.

Awakening your true power will allow you to use this force for healing wounds, embracing yourself, and helping others. You'll notice that other people will see the change of your energy, even if they can't exactly put their finger on what has changed.

Your vibrations will be peaking and transcending the low plateaus, which may surprise you. You're probably not used to feeling the intense glow of your inner light yet. As time goes by, you'll find yourself becoming more comfortable in higher plateaus as your body and soul adapt to the higher vibrations. Live your life as a child of the divine, and never create a rift between your soul and body by trying to hide your spirituality and higher vibrations.

The Akashic Records will finally give you a chance to relinquish the harsh and restrictive limitations that have been placed on you by a world filled with illusions. The Akashic Records are never exclusive to one part of our spirituality. Instead, they involve our past, current, and future lives as one, interconnected through multiple planes of energy. One strong wound can be buried deep enough to span several lifetimes. Healing one's self through Akashic Records ensures that spiritual wounds aren't healed superficially.

Since we're living in a world that's hyper-focused on survival, it's hard to find room to be able to focus on one's spirituality. Therefore, you should use the methods mentioned in the book when you're completely sure that you'll be able to pour all your attention into accessing the Akashic Records. It may be hard to accustom yourself during your early trials, but once you truly see for yourself how effective the Akashic Records are, you'll be able to easily find the concentration needed.

Whether it's addiction, loss, relationships, or spiritual fatigue that you're trying to heal or fix, look it in the eyes through accessing the Akashic Records. All the solutions you find in the Records are personal and unique, and this information won't work on someone else's problems, but you can still help others access their Akashic Records and find their own solutions. You may initially fear the radical transformation that can happen from using the information in the Akashic Records, but it shouldn't take you a lot of time to rejoice in happiness after fully understanding it.

Part 2: Twin Flames

The Ultimate Guide to Attracting Your Twin Flame, Signs You Need to Know and the Different Stages, Includes a Comparison of Relationships with Soul Mates and Life Partners

Introduction

Have you ever felt a connection with someone so strong that it was like a bolt of lightning coursing through your body? Did you ever meet someone, and after only five minutes of talking to them, you felt like you had known them for a lifetime? We all form connections with the people around us every day. Some will be a glancing moment and forgotten in minutes, while others will stay with us forever. Are those people meant to play a significant role in your life, or should you forget them and move on?

We are constantly being told there is a person out there who is "the one," but is that true? Is it possible that out of the billions of people on the planet, there is only one person who will become our perfect partner? With twin flames, then yes, there is a special connection out there waiting for you. Soulmates, however, are different, and life partners... Well, that's another story!

Maybe you believe, maybe you don't. This book will give you the knowledge you need to identify why certain people affect you in various ways. If you have soul mates or twin flames, surely life is perfect from the first time you meet? If this was true, then life would be much easier, but even the most tumultuous relationship can benefit from some insight into the journey they are on.

Chapter 1: What are Twin Flames?

If you have ever met someone who changed your life completely, they may have been your twin flame. When you form a high-level spiritual connection with someone, it can lead to love, friendship, or a combination of the two feelings. If you have a relationship with someone who is intense, life-enhancing, and spiritual, this could be a twin flame relationship that will endure any obstacles or circumstances.

To understand the concept better, go back to the origins of the twin flame theory. When you know the reasoning behind the doctrine, you understand more about the connection formed with your missing twin flame.

The History of the Twin Flame Theory

When considering the origins of twin flame theory, you can go back as far as history records allow. Nearly all civilizations have examples of separation of souls, yet Plato, the Greek philosopher, presents the most distinctive explanation of how humanity became divided to form two parts of the same soul.

Plato lived in the Classical period of Ancient Greece and formed a school of thinking simply known as Platonist. He composed a dialogue known as the Symposium in which he explained how the actions of the gods affected humankind and why the actions were necessary.

Originally humans had four arms, four legs, and two sets of genitalia. Their head comprised two faces, and there were three genders of humans. The traditional male and female were two of the genders, while the third was a hermaphroditic being with both sets of genitalia. In the Symposium, Plato stated these original humans were essential sources of labor and energy for the gods and other dwellers of the Higher Dimensions but were quickly becoming powerful beings. They threatened the gods, and it is written that the eradication of humans was considered.

Realizing this would leave the gods with no form of subjects to do their will, Zeus came up with a solution to increase the workforce while diminishing their strength. He separated the original human forms into halves. Each human then became the form we recognize today with two arms and legs with just one face and one set of genitalia.

While the process doubled the number of humans, it also weakened their power. The gods had created a form of slave that knew no pleasure and lacked the will to live. Humans starved themselves and died off, leaving the gods with a conundrum to solve. Apollo devised a solution, and that was to sew the original humans together and then divide them with a common bond, so they had a sense of purpose and desire. He reconstructed the human form with a belly button that became the redeeming sign that our twin flame still existed somewhere in the world.

Each human then became reborn. They were refueled with a desire to seek their twin flame and form a reconstituted version of their original self. The gods recognized that desire and emancipation made humans function on a higher level, yet the reality of them finding their twin flame was remote. This suited their purpose because when humans find their mirror image, they become a powerful force that rivals the beings that govern them, the gods themselves!

The Archetypical Example of a Twin Flame Relationship

Classical Greek history also gives us an example of the sacred lover archetype, Aphrodite, and Ares.

Ares is the divine male twin flame and the god of war. Aphrodite is his twin feminine flame and is also the goddess of love and beauty. They should have been repulsed by each other as they represent polar opposites with their beliefs and powers. Aphrodite was married to a powerful but ugly god called Hephaestus, who neglected his beautiful and frustrated wife by spending his nights in the workshop. Ares and Aphrodite took advantage of the situation and met to make love until dawn every evening.

It has been well reported that the Greek gods encouraged affairs with other people; they didn't encourage any form of fidelity. When the god Helios caught the lovers in a flagrant position, the story of their love enraged the gods, and they punished the lovers by separating them for eternity. These twin flames would not be kept apart by rules, and even following the godly declaration, they met regularly and produced seven children from their union! The god of Eros, whose powers include love, youthful magic, and sex, was one of these children and serves as a powerful reminder of what can happen when twin flames procreate.

Some people believe that it automatically means you will become romantically involved when you meet a twin flame. While this can be true, your twin flame could be a friend, a mentor, or even a student. They will often enter our lives when we are desperate for help. They form intense relationships that help us to steer through times of need. Twin flames will form relationships so intense it is uncommon for them to be lifelong relationships, so separation is sometimes inevitable.

It's okay for twin flame relationships to end, considering such levels of intensity can be unhealthy. When twin flames separate, it is painful, but the two people are left with crucial answers to life lessons and a feeling they have encountered their cosmic partner.

Are You Already Part of a Twin Flame Relationship?

Do you have a yin to your yang? Do you have a relationship with someone who completes you?

Here are some of the most common signs you are already connected to a twin flame:

1) Time is irrelevant to both of you. You can spend hours with each other and never get restless or bored. You both wonder where the time has gone, yet you feel ready to do it all again the following day.

2) Déjà vu: During conversations, you discover strange coincidences in your present and former experiences. It seems like life is forming a path, so you both reach each other. You are destined to have a relationship.

3) You both feel a magnetic force that crackles when you meet. You feel a connection between your physical and spiritual energies, and you form an unspoken understanding.

4) Your strengths make a perfect foil for their weaknesses and vice versa. Together you are a force to be reckoned with and are virtually unbeatable.

5) You have a shared sense of purpose. The ideas you hold dearest are a shared value you both strive to achieve.

6) As twins, you know each other inside out, flaws and all, and never judge each other.

7) You will disagree because you are comfortable that you will always resolve your differences, no matter how often you fall out.

8) You are connected on many levels. You may be partners, friends, shoulders to cry on, or mentors to each other.

9) You have synchronicity in your former lives. Sometimes you discover uncanny parallels in your personal history; for instance, you may have both been in the same place during a historic event like 9/11 without realizing it.

10) You grow as a couple and become more sympathetic, forgiving, and empathetic to others.

Why We Need Twin Flame Relationships

Contrary to some beliefs, we are a complete being even without this spiritual coupling. We all have a complete soul that can be strengthened by our own experiences, but a twin flame relationship helps you reach another level. These relationships help you shed all egos, understand what your hearts need to heal, and take the first steps to become a spiritually enhanced human.

The purpose behind your relationship with your twin flame can take many courses, but it will inevitably lead to a harmonious and balanced coupling with a positive outcome. This can include raising children, forming a bond especially important when it comes to ecological matters, doing business with each other, or becoming a spiritual mentor to each other.

Sometimes you can miss the signs that lead you to your twin flame. Outside influences may leave you feeling incapable of receiving the gift of a spiritual relationship and leave us unreceptive to the connection. You can be overwhelmed with emotions that leave you drained and flat, so you miss recognizing the signs you are in the presence of a twin flame. Maybe you are grieving or trapped in a bad relationship. When you may need spiritual help, the emotional points may be the reason you're failing to acknowledge their presence.

It doesn't matter if you seek a new spiritual connection or are simply meeting new people; it is essential to know how people make you feel. This can also apply to individuals we already live with or have in our life. They could be part of your spiritual makeup without you realizing the fact!

15 Things to Look for When You Meet a Potential Twin Flame

1) You always come away from spending time with them feeling like you've learned something. If you meet someone for the first time and feel like they can teach you something without you feeling inadequate or incompetent, then you may have encountered a twin flame. If you also feel like you have shared knowledge that could be world-changing, this could be your spiritual twin flame!

2) You immediately feel like this person is a safe place for you to go. When you meet someone who is completely trustworthy and will guard your secrets and thoughts, this can feel like coming home.

3) You know they will never judge you or reject you. This doesn't mean they won't be truthful with you or fail to pull you up when you mess up. They are so confident in your relationship they are probably the only person to tell you the whole truth with clarity that most people lack. They aren't afraid that you can't handle the truth, and they know how to work with you to become the better person you both know lies below the surface.

4) You never have to put a show on for them. If you feel awful, then you can act like it, and they will know exactly what to do. They will never berate you for having human emotions, but they will accompany you on the journey these emotions take you on.

5) You both have dark and light sides that complement each other. When your dark side is prevalent, they will display their light side to create a balanced, harmonious feeling. They instinctively know what mood you are in and how to be sympathetic to your aura.

6) You fall in love unconditionally. Every person loves another person or persons, such as parents and friends, past lovers or people who played an important part in their life, but falling in love is different. Twin flames fall in love despite convention and circumstances dictating it is wrong. They are unaffected by reality and any form of mental clarity. The heart wants this relationship, and it is a natural progression for both people.

7) You become scared of the relationship and want to bail. In the early stages of a twin flame relationship, you can feel overwhelmed by your emotions' intensity and depth. People can reach for their mental sneakers and withdraw. Imagine the coyote and roadrunner, and you get what this can look like. They are crazy, running around as one chases the other before quickly turning and becoming the one being pursued. We will discuss this aspect of twin flame relationships further into the book.

8) You don't feel threatened by spending time apart. You know that when you are together, you are bonded and form a single unit, but you still have your sense of freedom. Twin flame relationships shouldn't feel like they are smothering you; they should be strong enough to last, even when you aren't together. If you meet someone who is the

embodiment of everything you want, yet you are never anxious about being apart, they could be your twin flame.

9) You are finely tuned to each other's energy. If you have a spiritual connection, you immediately know how the other person is feeling. You know with just a glance when they are happy, sad, angry, or upset, and you know they can feel the same level of empathy towards you.

10) You feel a sense of completion. If you have been waiting for someone your entire life, you will know immediately that your search is over. Everybody knows that journeys can be arduous, especially when they are undefined by time. That relentless searching for a feeling of togetherness will stop once you meet your twin flame. You will experience a feeling of arrival at your destination, and you will happily step off the path of discovery.

11) You will be a mirror for their fears and desires. For example, if you are a creative soul who can create art and beauty with any medium, then your twin flame will probably be repressed and more likely to have no interest in the creative arts. If you are a messy, disorganized soul, then your twin flame will be a neat freak who demands high levels of the organization. If you are a dramatic character who overreacts in stressful situations, he or she will be a strong and willful partner who knows how to talk you down.

12) Your relationship with your twin flame will highlight how shallow your other relationships have been. When you connect with your twin flame, you will feel a depth and intensity you have never felt before. This doesn't mean that former relationships are irrelevant; after all, every relationship we have should teach us something. It merely highlights that spiritual connections are far more intense than physical or familial relationships ever can be.

13) You can't think of a single thing you would change about them. There are no rose-colored glasses in a twin flame relationship, and you both understand how the other person ticks. The difference is you embrace the flaws along with the qualities you both bring to the table. You know that as a unit, you are spectacular, and you don't want to change a thing! You may both be at different spiritual stages, but your prime objective is to help each other reach a higher level and discover your purpose.

14) There is no sense of competition. If you have a twin flame relationship, you will have a healthy respect for each other. You will celebrate their successes just as they celebrate yours. There is no room for envy and resentment when it comes to life success levels. You may be more or less successful than your twin, but it is never a problem. You aren't competing; you are striving to become better as a couple.

15) They will be ready to commit fully to your relationship. This doesn't just apply to romantic relationships, as the word commitment can apply to all forms of unions. When a friend commits to another friend, it means they will be there for them no matter what. You know whom you can trust to have your back and who is just a friend of convenience. Friends should come in all forms of commitment levels; the trick is to recognize them. Your twin flame will cross rivers and mountains to come to your side whenever you need them, and they will stand by your side no matter what.

The key part to understanding what twin flames are and how they affect your life is to remember that forces bigger than all of us are in force. You may not be ready to connect, but it is still essential to understand the signs that show you when the opportunity presents itself. Your twin may be unreceptive because they aren't at a stage in their life to meet you. Hold tight because your time will come, and meanwhile, you will gain the experience of how to analyze the other people you have in your life and your relationships with them.

Chapter 2: Soulmates vs. Twin Flame

What are the differences between these types of relationships? You already know something about what a twin flame brings to a relationship, so what do soulmates mean to you?

What are Soulmates?

They are people who will enter your life and influence it deeply. They are aligned to your soul and may even have been a major part of your former life. Just like twin flames, they will mirror you to some extent, and when you look at them, you can see your own weaknesses and strengths. However, the difference between soul mates and twin flames is the depth of the connection.

You have only one twin flame who is the embodiment of the other half of your soul, while your soulmates are extensions of your spiritual being. You will meet many soulmates in your life, and they will come in different forms. They will come into your life to shake things up and make your life more meaningful. They may form romantic attachments, or they may be friends who make your life more enjoyable.

Sometimes, the term *soulmate* can put pressure on a relationship. If one person describes the other as a soulmate, it's daunting to live up to that expectation. True soulmates should have easier relationships than others and have a natural flow without dark or difficult aspects. They are intense but joyful compared to twin flame relationships, which will often be torrid and filled with extreme emotions. Your soulmate should make you feel close to them and comfortable in their company.

Soulmates may come into your life for long periods and be around as a rock for you, or they may be the catalyst that sparks an idea and then departs from your life in a matter of minutes. Soulmates have a give and take relationship, and they will sometimes push you outside of your comfort zone when needed. Soulmates are meant to teach us life lessons and improve our spiritual strength. They will help you raise your spiritual consciousness while twin flame relationships work together to raise the entire world's spiritual consciousness.

You will meet many soulmates during your time on earth, yet you may never meet a twin flame. That's not meant to be a statement that should make you feel sad. Your twin flame is a special part of your soul, but you don't have to connect with them to have a successful and fulfilled life. You are complete as you are, but if you are blessed with a twin flame connection, then you will work together to create intense energy that can be arduous and painful yet filled with the most intense love.

The Signs You Have Met Someone From Your Soul Group

Your soul group comprises people with whom you have a natural connection. You will connect with them on a mental, emotional, physical, and spiritual level without knowing why. The energy between you will resonate so strongly it may feel physical. Soulmates create strong bonds that can transcend time and create vibrations that will create harmony within the group.

Soulmates within your soul group can be from different backgrounds, cultures, and gender and will often have diverse backgrounds that bear no relation to your own. What they do have in common is a strong sense of shared values and dreams. They believe in the same things you do, and they share the same principles and ethics as you.

You need to be open to meeting members of your soul group to benefit from the experience. They are all sent into your life to help you grow and move past fear, but if negative attitudes bog you down, you will not enjoy meeting members of your soul group. Many spiritual traditions believe that the obstacles we face in life are predetermined even before we are born. The people who enter your life as part of your soul group are chosen to help you overcome these obstacles and grow as a spiritual being.

Where Do You Meet People from Your Soul Group?

This is one of the most important questions you can ask, and others will tell you to search everywhere. Although, if you chose to take that approach, it can take over your life. Your spiritual path is preordained, and the chance to meet your soul group will present itself when you are ready. That doesn't mean you should sit back and go about your normal routine changing nothing; after all, you can't win the lottery if you don't purchase a ticket! Once you feel your soul group's synchronicity pulling you in, you need to be ready to embrace the feelings and seek them out.

This process involves allowing your heart to rule your head and listening to your gut feelings. Your headspace will be filled with all your fears and safety measures that instinctively guide you on a safe and comfortable path. Your heart, meanwhile, is more inclined to take you out of your comfort zone and take a new path. Try following your intuition instead of your tried and tested methods of living. Embrace new experiences and the related opportunities they present.

When you want to meet new people and broaden your horizons, the Internet may seem like the last place to start. Online interaction is not something you would associate with finding your soulmate, but it is the perfect starting point. You can research new subjects, hobbies, and interests to discover your potential soulmates.

Create an online course for people in your area interested in the same things you are. A meetup course for cooking or art could mean you will meet like-minded people who may just be part of your soul group. Even if you don't find a soulmate immediately, you will establish new connections and increase your social group, which is always positive.

The local church can be a perfect way to meet people and become an active part of the community. Volunteer work is also hugely rewarding and gives you a sense of giving back to the community. It's true that as we get older, it is more difficult to make friends and form new relationships, so you need to put the effort in and say yes to new experiences. Stop checking out online contacts and liking photos from remote friends and concentrate on the people you encounter every day.

How Do You Know When You Have Met Someone from Your Soul Group?

1) **Your Eye Contact is Intense:** When you look into someone's eyes and feel a connection that is familiar and comfortable, then you may have met a soulmate. They have a coupling with your soul that can feel ancient and unbroken, and it will never feel uncomfortable.

2) **They Will be Soul-Centric:** Members of your soul group won't be interested in your social statuses, such as how much money you have, your status at work, or other ego-centric parts of your life. They will be more interested in your spiritual footprint on the world. Expect conversations about environmental issues and conscious living as you begin to share your common interests.

3) You Will Feel a Magnetic Pull: Even if your meeting is brief, you will be mesmerically drawn to them and their energy.

4) You Share the Same Beliefs: Members of your soul group will often amaze you with their synchronicity to your beliefs. They will be on the same page and will often mirror your words and thoughts.

5) You Have a Timeless Relationship with Them: From the minute you meet a soulmate, you are comfortable in their company. You don't have an initial awkwardness or reservation. You could have known this person for the whole of your life.

6) They Appear at the Most Opportune Moment: You may be unaware of your personal sense of attachment, but members of your soul group will instinctively know you are ready to meet them. There are numerous types of soul connections in your soul group, and they will appear to you when you need them the most.

7) Time is Irrelevant: You could spend hours with soul mates and never notice where the time went. It's like the clock that governs your thoughts and actions has temporarily stopped working. You are so immersed in your connection you feel that nothing else matters, and you refuse to be distracted by life!

8) They Will Challenge You Without Condemnation: Your soul group is there to make you grow as a person and as a spiritual being. They love to challenge you and push you towards circumstances that will test your life skills and emotions. They will never abandon you and will always know the correct level of support you need at any given time.

9) Your Soul Will Feel Energized: When you have an encounter with one of your soul groups, you will come away with a feeling of nourishment. It will feel as if your soul has just had the best meal ever and is full and contented.

10) You Can be Yourself: Your soul group is aware of your true personality. You will never need to be fake or pretend to feel things you don't. The authentic you can rise to the surface and breathe deeply around your soul mates, and they will never judge you.

The 10 Types of Soul Mates

Your soul group comprises multiple types of mates, so it is important to realize who can be part of our spiritual consciousness and common humanity.

1) Soul Partners: These are the most common types of connections and are formed with people you agree to partner with. Most people associate this type of soul mate with marriage and raising a family, but there are many other types of partnerships to which we can commit. Forming a company with someone can lead to a connection that makes them part of your soul group, or it can be as simple as a beloved sibling who is your life partner. Nobody can travel through life alone, and our soul partners are here to remind us how intricately human lives are weaved together.

2) Reincarnated Soul Mates: When souls reconnect in this life, it can mean they have unresolved issues from their past lives. They can also signify that the souls have spent countless lifetimes together. Whatever the case, this type of connection is one of the most powerful in your soul group, but you need to take precautions with the relationship. Try to disregard any residual feelings you have from past lives and judge each other on the person you are in this life. You may need to heal rifts and then let them go so both your souls can heal.

3) Romantic Soul Mates: This can be the same as a soul partner, or it can be an opportunity to grow with the relationship. Everyone knows that romance is not the only ingredient in a successful relationship, and these connections are not always meant to be long lasting. Romantic soulmates help us grow as a person and take the rough with the smooth. They may cause you devastating wounds or challenge you with their behavior, but they are fulfilling a purpose. They are teaching you how to form successful relationships, even if it isn't with them.

4) Companion Soul Mates: Imagine a life in which all your relationships were romantic, or family-based. That would be hell, right? Who would you turn to when you need advice or support from someone removed from interpersonal relationships? Your companion soul mate or mates provide you with the support group you need to keep going on your earthly odyssey. If your life were written in a novel form, some people would describe soul companions as your spiritual sidekicks. They may be in your life for a couple of months or decades; it doesn't matter. They are the food and drink your soul needs, and they provide companionship for your spirit.

5) Soul Families: These are not your actual physical family, but they are just as important. People worldwide who show the same passion as you do for particular causes or activities can be part of your soul family. Spiritual groups actively working to bring love and peace to our planet may never meet each other, but they will feel connected because of the depth of their commitment to the cause.

6) Kindred Spirits: These connections can be formed by a commonality that leads to shared experiences. They aren't always soul mates, but they are important to you and your life. Maybe you both have similar life experiences that strengthen your bond. Young mothers struggling with their newborn babies will turn to kindred spirits in the same situation. People in the same profession may become part of your soul group because they understand the tensions and stress your career involves. It can be incredibly satisfying to spend time with a soul who just gets what you are about.

7) Soul Contract: This is not really a part of your soul group but rather a contract you make with yourself. You become another member of your soul group and promise yourself to do something monumental in this lifetime. You may make this connection with someone else or with yourself, just knowing the depth of commitment will help you when struggling to reach your objective is inspirational and soul lifting.

8) Soul Teachers: These members of your soul group are sent to educate you. They may be traditional relationships you form with educators who help you through school or college, or they may be more diverse. When you form a relationship with a person who can guide the path your life will take, it can be magical. College professors or counselors can be soul mates who aren't just educating you; they show you how important your advice and counsel can be for others further down the line. They are sharing the gift of knowledge and the importance of sharing it.

9) Soul Crossings: You may feel that the most important part of your soul group is the people who are there for you throughout your life and are constant companions. This can be true sometimes, but the fleeting meetings we have with soul mates can be just as important. The phrase "ships that pass in the night" is the perfect way to describe these encounters. You may feel an intense connection, but the time and place aren't right for long-term relationships. This could be someone you meet on holiday and form an immediate bond with, but you lose touch when you return home. Or a lover you meet who has been diagnosed with a terminal illness and passes away a month after you meet.

The point of these connections is to help you understand that time is irrelevant concerning connections of the soul. They are all essential and teach us something, even if they are brief.

10) Karmic Soul Mates: What do you think karma is? Is it a system of punishment and reward where the universe deals out karma depending on our actions? Karma is a natural energy governed by cause and effect, and the members of your soul group that are karmic soul mates will help you grow and evolve. They enter your life at key moments and facilitate you to change direction. They may be positive influencers who will help your soul evolve, or they may be negative forces who will help you recognize when life is taking you down the wrong path.

Our soul group provides the support and encouragement needed to get through life. Remember that your soul is always craving new experiences and looking to evolve. Recognizing the people who form part of your soul group will help you facilitate this evolution.

So, what is the difference between soul mates and twin flames? You have multiple soul mates and just one twin flame. The depth of intensity will be off the scale when you meet your twin flame, and it has been described as a "soul mate on crack!"

Chapter 3: Twin Flames as Life Partners

When we consider archetypal love relationships and how people describe their partners, the term "life partner" is often used. It creates an image of two people who meet, fall in love, create a family, and then grow old together. Life partners are meant to be there for each other through thick and thin.

So, with this in mind, is it ideal to have a twin flame as a life partner? In most cases, the answer is a definite no. Twin flames are two parts of the same soul and turbulently connect with passionate and highly charged emotions involved. You can't choose your twin flame; you are joined on a spiritual level. If you are destined to meet, you will. Twin flames will often push you into a dark place and force you to rethink how you function as an individual.

Twin flames enter your life to make you a stronger individual and take you to your highest highs and your lowest lows. The blind passion you feel for them will not always be sexual, but you will love them with an unhealthy level of toxicity, and people around you will often warn you to get out of the relationship. When you connect with your twin flame, you will feel like an addict. You crave the connection you have, and it is more important to you than all your other relationships.

Soulmates are also a predestined kind of connection. You have shared experiences, possibly from past lives, and they are often guided into your life to serve a purpose. When you need a soulmate, they can appear in any type of relationship. They may stick around or be gone once they have fulfilled their purpose; relationships with soulmates are not always about longevity.

So, what is the difference between these two love relationships and life partners? All the relationships you have had before you meet your life partner are designed to help you recognize the qualities you need in your choice of a life partner. The spiritual wounds and heartbreak you have suffered in the past are all part of the process that leads you to your ideal life partner. This connection is not just about romantic relationships, and they can occur in different aspects of life.

The more you accept love into your life, then you will be ready to accept a plethora of life partners who will make you a more rounded individual with strong relationships to keep you grounded.

Definitiveŀ Types of Life Partnerships You Should be Looking For:

> **1) Partner:** A great way to start is with the most traditional form of a life partner, your significant other. It may be a boyfriend, girlfriend, husband, or wife. Your definition of a partner doesn't matter; the term life partner transcends gender, sexuality, or fluidity.
>
> We all seek love, protection, and the need for a safe relationship we can call on to retreat to when the world is proving to be a bit too challenging. A life partner will be there for you when you need them and step up to the plate when you need them. Traditionally this involves the male partner taking a "hero" role with their woman. They will step

in and rescue their partner just like the heroic male they are biologically programmed to be, but the modern world has moved on, and women are more likely to play a different role than traditional heroes and damsels. They will expect to be just as protective as their male counterparts and be there for them whenever they are needed.

Does this mean that the hero instinct should be ignored? No, it shouldn't! It is built into male DNA, and they often need to feel some heroic role to keep the relationship healthy.

Here are a few simple ways females can keep their men feeling like heroes without seeming like a bimbo!

- **Make Sure They are Satisfied in the Bedroom:** Men are naturally programmed to keep their women happy in bed, so even if you aren't fully engaged because you are tired or not in the mood, don't make them feel inadequate. Act like you can't keep your hands off them, which is hopefully true, and tell them exactly what you love about them. Experiment between the sheets and have just as much fun planning new positions or places to try them. The best way to make men walk tall is to let them know they are keeping you happy in bed!

- **Ask for Assistance:** We all want to feel equal in our relationships, but certain tasks suit men physically. Choose the tasks that suit your strengths and ask him to help you with others. Let him open those tricky jars or help you carry stuff from the car. Why would anybody struggle with stuff when they have someone who will willingly do it for them?

- **Share Decisions:** Modern women are so often in control of their own lives that when they enter a relationship, they just naturally take over the decision-making process. This can be emasculating for men, but they will often choose a quiet life rather than assert themselves. Women must share major decisions like where to go on vacation or which place to book for dinner. Ask him for his opinion, and you will avoid any simmering resentment, and you may even be pleasantly surprised at his input!

2) Mentor: This role is typical of a different form of a life partner. They will be the rock you lean on when you need advice that is practical and from the heart. Some people mistakenly expect their romantic life partner to fill all the roles in their lives, and this pressures the relationship and can cause it to fall apart. This life partner can have played a significant part in your education, maybe a lecturer or teacher at school or college who has guided you to the path you are on.

It could be a person in the workplace who has taken you under their wing and shared their knowledge with you. Mentors come in all shapes and sizes, and some will be there for you throughout your life while others may bow out. Even those who have left are classed as life partners. They haven't left the relationship due to toxicity or disagreement and can be called upon for advice whenever needed.

3) Anchor: Whom do you turn to when your life hits a speed bump, or you need someone to turn to when your relationship is in turmoil? Your anchor is the person who will be there for you when you need help, no matter what the time or circumstance. You trust this person and have chosen them to be your life partner because of their intuitiveness and level of thinking. This is not a relationship where your anchor will agree with you on all levels and back you up; this is a relationship that will help you consider all sides. They will play the devil's advocate and suggest different ways to go for you in the future. Anchors will ground you and help you set achievable priorities in your life.

4) Confidante: This type of life partner is the one you tell your deepest, darkest secrets to. You know this relationship is unbreakable, and your secrets are safe with your confidante. You know you can talk to them in ways that others may find shocking. You can share how you really feel about the woman at work who everybody loves, and you don't understand why. Your confidante won't judge you or call you out for being nasty. They will probably have some equally cutting things to say about the people you know that will have you both in fits of laughter. Having a person with whom you can be as mean as you like helps you keep the rancor out of your "normal" life. We all need to let off steam now and then, and your confidante understands this.

The main difference between soul mates, twin flames, and life partners is all about the connection you form. Soul mates and twin flames will automatically know you; they understand what drives you and how your spiritual being functions. Life partners need to learn about you. You are forming a relationship with life partners without the same history as soul mates and twin flames.

You won't feel a deep level connection immediately; in fact, it may never occur, and that's not a bad thing. Deep spiritual relationships often come with baggage. There are intense emotions involved both in this life and previous ones, which can affect both partners. These connections are designed to test your boundaries and will often cause intense pain and heartache.

Life partners are people you have a lot in common with, and you feel a depth of love just as important but needs to grow. Spiritual connections are more like a jolt of energy that is unexplained and can rock you to the core of your being. Life partners generate a love like a plant; it needs to be fed and watered and will grow as time progresses. If treated correctly and nurtured, it will bloom and flower while providing you with strong roots, and you will see the fruits of your labor.

Perhaps the most significant thing to remember about a life partner is that you will have a choice. Twin flames and soul mates have a predestined part to play in your life, so balance it out with your life partners. They represent your personality and life choices and mirror the values and qualities you hold.

Remember that a twin flame and soul mate will often cause you pain, and that's okay. Yet, it is also the main reason you will need to break contact with them at some point. A life partner is someone you have spent your life with, and you trust they will not cause you pain, although some probably will.

27 Traits to Look for in a Life Partner

1) A Strong Sense of Who They Are and What They Want: You need someone complete. When you form a relationship with a life partner, they need to be in the right frame of mind to become committed. If your life partner needs you to define them, then you probably will spend all your time propping them up, and that's not healthy.

2) Honesty: We all tell white lies and know how to bend the truth with our partners. Should you tell them just how much you hate their new hairstyle or outfit? No, you use tact and diplomacy to save hurting their feelings, and that's part of being a decent partner. Lying is different. The minute your partner tells you a lie, you lose trust and respect.

3) Delight: You need to feel a sense of joy when you see this person. If you feel anything other than total pleasure in their company, then they shouldn't become part of your life partnership team.

4) Morality: Choose life partners that believe in the same moral code as you, and you won't be disappointed by your choice. Never compromise on the principles you both have. It's okay to have different beliefs and goals, but you should share the same level of integrity.

5) Responsibility: You need to choose people who are just as accountable for your life as they are for theirs. They need to be willing to invest in you and be there when you need them.

6) A Shared Sense of Humor: Everybody has different things that make them laugh, but you do need a life partner with whom you can share funny stuff. Make sure they don't take themselves too seriously and can laugh at life. You will need that shared humor when times get tough.

7) Inner Strength: When you are feeling weak or vulnerable, you need to know they have the strength to prop you up. This can be a strength physically present - as well as mental strength. Sometimes you just need to be the one being looked after and embrace it!

8) Ability to Trust: Some people are unwilling to lean on others and find it hard to trust other people. A balanced relationship means that both partners can be strong ones whenever the need arises. Your life partner needs to be in a position they can trust you to take the lead.

9) Maturity: You must be both at the same point of emotional development in a loving relationship. Mentors and anchors can be different, but you both need to be adults in a loving relationship. Immaturity is not an attractive quality in your life partner, and it will soon become a problem if your partner becomes an adolescent in your relationship.

10) Compatibility: This should be evident from the first day you meet. If you clash over simple things, then the chance of forming a successful life partner relationship is slim. You can't work on your reciprocity because it is a fundamental part of the relationship.

11) Independence: A successful relationship means that spending time apart isn't a problem. Life partners should have separate interests and hobbies and realize that independence should be a part of who you are. Never give up your identity to become part of a couple. Your identity should be what makes you so attractive to your life partner and a major reason they love spending time with you.

12) The Same Level of Commitment: Avoid people wary of commitment. A relationship will only grow when you are both on the same page. This doesn't mean you need to take things too quickly, but you need to know that a life partner won't bail on you once the level of commitment is raised.

13) Vulnerability: If someone has their emotional walls up, then you won't be able to form a fulfilling relationship with them. Humans are naturally vulnerable, and while it is essential to have barriers, you also need to know when to let them down. This applies to partners as well; how can you get close to someone who is impenetrable?

14) Ability to Debate: While life partners may not be as contentious as twin flames or soul mates, differences will inevitably occur. You need to know that your potential life partner can thrash things out so it suits you both. If they tend to sulk or shout without resolving problems, then you will both become frustrated when arguing.

15) Humility: While self-assurance is a quality that can be incredibly attractive, self-centeredness is less attractive. Humility is essential in a life partner; after all, if they are incapable of admitting their mistakes, you will be blamed for things for which you aren't responsible.

16) Affection: Some people are comfortable with public displays of emotion, while others are more discreet. Both attitudes are fine, but make sure your potential life partner has the same attitude as you do. If your life partner is keen to hold hands and kiss in public, but you aren't, it will lead to problems. Similarly, if you need affection and they are unwilling to give it, you will feel neglected.

17) Empathy: Life partners are there for you, so the ability to show empathy is essential. They may not fully understand what you are going through, but they should be able to comfort you and make you feel better.

18) A Balanced Sense of Ambition: When you form a loving life partnership, you need to be clear about what you expect from the relationship. For instance, if one of you is content to live in a comfy family home and work a regular 40-hour week to pay the bills and the other one wants to be the C.E.O. of his own company and is willing to work 18-hour days, then it can cause conflict. Some couples will make it work, but they need to know what lies in store for the future and any concessions they need to consider.

19) A Healthy Attitude to Relationships: This doesn't mean they have to show a perfect dating history; after all, relationships take many forms. They need to have a sense of family, whatever that means to them. It could be their relationship with their actual family or the bonds they have with co-workers. The main thing to watch out for is people who have no relationships; this isn't normal and can be a red flag regarding their ability to form new relationships.

20) Open-Mindedness: Nobody wants an inflexible partner. You need to know you will grow as a partnership and embrace new ideas and experiences.

21) Faithfulness: Without fidelity, a loving relationship will fail. Even if both parties commit to an "open" relationship, the cracks will appear quickly. You need to know that when your partner is somewhere else, they are still faithful to you.

22) Mutual Sexual Attraction: Loving life partnerships often thrive better with a healthy dose of lust thrown into the mix! You need to know that the attraction you feel is mutual, and you both want to rip each other's clothes off at any given time. You also understand that you will feel the same way even when your potential partner feels unattractive because of illness, for example.

23) Curiosity: A naturally inquisitive nature is part of a successful life partnership because you both know you won't tire of life any time soon. You want to choose someone who will be your willing partner in life's adventures and a perfect companion for the future.

24) Flexibility: You need to know that your potential life partner knows that life is full of opportunities, and sometimes they will need to drop what they are doing and roll with it! Life is a series of natural events and spontaneity. If you are too busy making plans, it will pass you by.

25) Forgiveness: Nobody is perfect, and you will make mistakes that will hurt each other. Your potential life partner needs to be a tolerant person who won't hold grudges and can forgive freely.

26) Enjoy Simple Pleasures: Life isn't filled with huge, monumental experiences; it is mostly mundane and uneventful. So, if your life partner is a positive soul who derives pleasure from everyday experiences and encounters, they will bring joy into your life. Sharing a piece of pizza or watching the sunset in the evening may not seem life-changing, but if they are enjoyed with your life partner, they can be unbeatable!

27) Communication: The cornerstone of all relationships. Your set of life partners should know how to reach you on every level. They should be articulate, knowledgeable, and great communicators because you need people who are eloquent and open to discourse.

Chapter 4: Stage 1: The Search

When you search for something, it can become a mission like no other. You may be searching for your perfect home, which means you spend all your time online checking out listings, visiting districts, or aimlessly driving around looking for real estate signs outside of properties. You know what you want and how to look for it, but the search can become all you think about. When that happens, you can neglect other areas of your life.

Perhaps you have experienced this type of obsession and think this is the perfect way to search for your twin flame. Well, the news is in, and searching for your twin flame is a process unlike any other you will experience. You aren't looking for a physical object or something that is essential for your daily life. You are looking for a spiritual connection with a part of your soul separated from you for many millenniums, and the chances you will reconnect are slim. Does that mean you shouldn't try? After all, if the percentages of your meeting are so low, why bother, right?

Of course, people will take a negative stance regarding the search for their twin flame, but if you decide to go for it, then you are opening the possibilities of the most fulfilling relationship of your life. You could experience the ultimate form of spiritual fireworks and the most intense emotions imaginable. Does that sound like it's worth looking for? Then let's level the playing field and make sure you are prepared for the first stage of twin flame development.

First, you must understand the concept of divine timing, as this is the process that governs the twin flame journey. Unfortunately, the way we have been taught to think and view the world conflicts with the concept of divine timing. If you can change the way you think and adopt healthier thoughts about the journey to find your twin flame, then the process will become less distressing.

Common Misconceptions About Divine Timing and How to Change Them

Misconception #1: You need to change yourself and your environment to allow divine timing to happen.

Consider how we view our normal physical world. What must we do to improve our situations and achievements? We must work harder and dedicate ourselves to the search for success. We must give 110% to everything we do, and only then can we expect to be rewarded for our efforts. We often think that our effort and dedication are the only way to achieve anything worth having. While this is true in the human world, the spiritual world is vastly different.

Cast off the 3-D concept and surrender yourself to the grace of divine timing. Allow the universe to dictate when things will happen and float on the flow of inevitability. Divine timing means you need to let go of the concept you control what happens next and just enjoy the gliding sensation of the current that is the universal flow.

How to Fix Misconception #1

- **Surrender Your Ego:** Self-confidence is an important part of our makeup, and it can help you achieve great things that seem impossible. The spiritual world is different; you need to become part of something larger than your ego. Stop demanding that certain things suit your time frame or in the manner you find acceptable. Stuff will happen when the universe decides, and nothing you can do can change that.

- **Stop the Belief that You Have Any Power Over the Universe:** The physical world may be your domain, but a higher force governs the spiritual world. Your twin flame journey will take the path it has been allocated, and no matter how strong your willpower, nothing will change that fact.

- **Change How You See the Term "Surrender":** What does the term "surrendering" mean? Is it a sign of weakness or giving up, or is it all about laying down your weapons and understanding that certain things are out of your control? Try putting a positive spin on surrendering and change how you think about it. Allow yourself to be open to faith, hope, and a belief that a beautiful life awaits those who embrace this concept.

Misconception #2: Divine timing is based on the conditional version of behavioral efforts and will always result in rewards.

For instance, as children, we were taught that:

- If you tidy your room, you can go play with your friends.

- If you eat all your greens, you can have ice cream as dessert.

- If you behave well during the year, Santa will put you on the "nice list," and you will get plenty of presents.

- If you do your homework, you can play games after.

This is known as the "if leads to then" approach and, when applied to the twin flame concept, means we think we need to "fix" ourselves before we are ready to enter the physical union of our two halves. Although you need to be in the right frame of mind and open to the experience for it to happen, that doesn't mean you need to "work" on yourself. The most important work you need to do to ready yourself for the experience is dropping rather than fixing. This will be covered later in this chapter.

How to Fix Misconception #2

- **Understand the Positivity of Divine Timing:** There are no punishment options in divine timing. You will always be supported on your journey, and the place you occupy on the journey is right even when it doesn't feel like it.
- **Have the Confidence That You Are Making Progress:** Your spiritual voyage is always advancing and will never backtrack. You may slow down and speed up as your spiritual evolvement blossoms, but you will never take steps backward.
- **Believe in the Universe:** Know that everything that happens on your spiritual path is happening *for you* and is benefitting you. Nothing is being done *to you* as a punitive measure. This concept is so different from the physical world; it's difficult to grasp. Think of it as life is your ultimate support system, and you will benefit from it for as long as you exist.

Misconception #3: Divine timing is a force that exists apart from our physical reality.

How do you believe we are governed on earth? Is there a vengeful force ready to smite us whenever we get it wrong? If you have been taught to follow popular religious ideals, then you are probably all too aware of the concept of a vengeful being that needs to be worshipped and obeyed. This leads to a belief you are powerless, and you need to please people and follow their doctrine.

Those who have been taught this, believe that the only way they can feel safe and accepted is when everybody around them is happy and content with their circumstances. This means everybody is seeking justifications for self-worth and looking to others to guide them on their journeys. You need to remember that you matter above all else and that divine timing is all about letting go of the "please others first" mentality.

How to Fix Misconception #3

Now is the time to clear your preconceived notions of how you think about your earthbound self and its connection to your spiritual self. When you reincarnate on earth, a significant portion of your soul remains in the spiritual realm.

A larger, all-loving, all-seeing portion of us remains outside of earthly reality and works hand in hand with the universe or the ultimate source of energy to coordinate the divine timing that governs your spiritual journey.

Your earthly self is governed by human doubts and restrictions, but in the spiritual realm, there is a bigger, more powerful part of your soul to bat for you every minute of every day. This spiritual part of you is the ultimate cheerleader for your physical you and will work tirelessly with the original source of energy to align you and on how to meet your twin flame.

This extended part of yourself knows all about the bigger picture and will help guide you to the point of greatness where you are prepared for what the universe has in store for you. Put your trust in this extended part of your soul and let it take control. It makes things so much easier when you know the nudges it gives you, and you recognize when your spiritual self is making a difference.

Personal Growth and How to Prepare Yourself for Your Twin Flame

Now you know how the spiritual world is geared up and ready to accompany you on your quest, it's time to get your physical self in the best form for the journey. This means you need to become the best version of yourself possible, both physically and mentally. You know that any future interaction with your twin flame will be demanding on your emotions and will create inner turmoil. This can affect your physical and spiritual health, so they both need to be at their best.

These suggestions are all about getting to know yourself inside and out. They encourage you to dive into personal development and embrace the process. This form of personal growth should never be considered a chore. Instead, it should be the ultimate way to get to know yourself from every angle.

1) **Create a Morning Routine:** When you wake up in the morning, you should be refreshed, filled with energy, and ready to face the world. Forming a routine means you are taking advantage of your elevated energy levels and making sure stuff gets done. Start with a healthy breakfast and a refreshing cup of herbal tea before you start your routine.

Try to include at least one self-care ritual like meditation or working out. Early morning routines are often the best time to clear out the clutter. So, start your day with positive actions by getting rid of some of the mess in your life. You will leave home feeling lighter and more organized.

2) **Absorb Information:** The modern world is a place filled with information. It can be overwhelming, but if you apply filters, you can learn something new every day. Information is power, and we all want to feel more powerful. You are growing spiritually, so take the time to grow as an individual. Read more books, join up for classes, or try a new sport. Even the least artistic people can create works of art. Painting, mosaics, pottery classes, or just doodling in a sketchbook all count as personal growth! Perhaps divine forces will inspire you to learn a new language because that is the mother tongue of your twin flame. Stranger things have happened!

3) Work Out Often: It doesn't matter what form your exercise takes; it just matters that you commit to it. Even 30 minutes a day is preferable to none! Get your body moving and release those precious endorphins that help your brain function more successfully. Not only will you feel better, it will also improve your sleep, your skin will feel healthier, and your body will feel the benefits almost immediately. Your self-confidence will be boosted, and you will just feel better overall!

4) Talk to Your Spiritual Self: You now know that much of your soul resides in the spiritual plane. Have a chat with this important part of yourself. Ask how it is and what it can teach you. Learn how to recognize the traditional ways the spiritual world connects with our earthly beings and what they are trying to tell you. The universe is not a subtle communicator! If you are open to communications, then you will get them! Any message they send will be loud and clear! For instance, if you are looking for a new job and appeal to your spiritual self for a hint, it will happen.

You may notice a stranger in your area who is appealing to you because of their style. You may love the car they drive or admire their style of dress. One day you will strike up a conversation with them when they mention a new company they work for who are currently hiring. In fact, they are hiring people for a position you would love. So, would you like the details and maybe a direct number you can phone? Of course, you would! This is an example of synchroneity and a clear sign the spiritual world is lending a hand.

5) Write a Letter to Your Twin Flame: While you recognize that a meeting isn't always going to happen, you are essentially connecting to them before you meet. Remember, they are the other half of your original soul, and you can ask whatever you like. How do you get to know people you are in a relationship with? You ask them questions and go on dates. So how do you get to know your twin flame or the other half of you?

You go on dates and ask questions. Since your twin flame is still a mystery, the best thing you can do is ask yourself the questions you would ask them. What are their/your ultimate goals? Who do they/you love most in this world? What type of experience brings them/you the most joy?

You get the idea. It may seem weird at first, but the process can be fun and revealing.

6) Forgive Yourself: This is a huge part of personal growth and can sometimes prove the most difficult. Hindsight is a beast for analyzing the past, and we can beat ourselves up over things that have happened, and we cannot change.

Here are a few common life mistakes you need to forgive yourself for:

- **Jobs You Didn't Take:** Most of us have made mistakes in our careers. Opportunities wasted or taking the wrong path are just a part of life. If you acted on your gut instinct when everything else suggested a different outcome, then you did the right thing. You will never know what would have happened if you had taken a different approach so let it go!

- **Money Matters:** If you find yourself in debt and struggling to cope with your finances, then do something about it instead of blaming yourself. Start with a frank conversation with your debtors and a practical plan to repay them. Being complacent and hiding your head in the sand will only lead to further regrets.

- **Friends You Have Hurt:** If you know that your actions have hurt somebody you care about, then try to make amends for your actions. Maybe it's too late for some people, so you need to walk away from the drama and commit to being a better friend in the future. Recognizing that you can improve is the first step to doing it!

- **Lost Love:** Relationships are a real kicker when it comes to regret. Many people find it difficult to get over relationships and move on to new ones. The road to new relationships should be free from obstacles and clear to travel. Remember, divine timing is guiding you, and it will help you realize when it's time to move on!

7) Eliminate the Toxic Elements of Your Life: Everywhere you look, you will find examples of how to declutter your life. All the so-called experts are telling you that if you have a clean closet, your life will automatically become better. While this is probably true, having a clean closet isn't really a major step for personal growth!

Applying the same principle to life is. Get rid of the things holding you back and stop being pushed backward by toxic relationships, habits, and environments.

Here are examples of toxic relationships you need to avoid:

- **The Controller:** Is there someone in your life who constantly tells you what to do? They tell you how to dress, where to go, and how to speak. Ditch them immediately and learn how to think for yourself.

- **The Downer:** Do you know someone who can find the negative aspects of even the most joyous event? Do they love misery and attempt to drain you of positivity? You know what to do! Get rid of them and surround yourself with positive energy instead.

- **The Perfectionist:** This can be a tricky one since we all need someone who encourages us to be a better person. Perfectionists will never be satisfied with your efforts and will fail to give you credit for any improvements. This will eventually lead to you feeling disheartened, so make sure you tell them their negative input isn't required anymore!

- **The Manipulator:** You know the type. They are masters at getting what they want while still making you feel bad about yourself. They know how to put an idea in your head that makes you do stuff you don't want and mess with your head. You don't want a game player; you want a game-changer!

- **The Competitor:** Healthy competition is great, and you should welcome it, but if you are in a relationship with an ultimate competitor who turns every situation into a battle, you will soon become drained of energy. You need people who will support you and be a team player, not someone who reduces your achievements to make themselves look better.

Chapter 5: Stage 2: The Awakening

The next natural stage of the twin flame process is the awakening, also known as the yearning. Because the experience involves two halves of the same soul, their timelines may differ. You may have worked on your spiritual growth and be prepared to meet your twin flame, yet they may be unaware of the need to begin their search. This explains why this stage is described as a period of yearning when you may feel a spiritual void. You know a part of you is missing, and you may look for different ways to compensate for that missing link.

Do You Use Relationships to Fill Your Spiritual Void?

As the song tells us, "All You Need Is Love," but are loving romantic relationships the best way to prepare for your twin flame? As you become more experienced in love matters, you may think that you will be better prepared for your twin flame connection. While you need to be in the best shape both physically and mentally for the meeting, nothing you experience beforehand can prepare you for the barrage of emotions you are about to undergo.

Immersing yourself in unsuitable relationships can make you less prepared to meet your twin flame. Be open to unconditional love and ready to experience the true sunshine of the spirit, and that won't happen if you are hampered by baggage from your previous relationships. It is human nature to seek a companion and benefit from the love and comfort they provide, but some people are too focused on "being in a relationship" rather than enjoying healthy relationships that occur naturally.

Do you feel the need to fill your spiritual void and lessen your yearning by being in a relationship? Here are some signs that indicate you may be using relationships to fill your void:

1) **You are Miserable When Single:** If you find yourself envying couples and feeling lost without a significant other, then you have a spiritual void. You need to be happy without being part of a couple. Try some following singular actions and embrace your singledom.

- **Travel Alone:** Go somewhere you have always wanted to visit. Choose somewhere you know you will love and create your own adventures!
- **Create Other Relationships:** Strengthen ties to your family and friends that may have weakened over time. We all grow apart from people, so maybe now is the time to reconnect.
- **Be Adventurous:** If you have ever held back certain parts of your personality because you were worried about how a partner would react, then embrace your weirdness and do stuff you have always wanted to. Karaoke in a local bar, roller-skating at the local skate park, driving a quad bike,

or taking a course about cooking sushi are all fun options. It doesn't matter what it is, just do it!

2) Your Mood Depends on Your Partner: Empathy is part of a healthy relationship, but it can also be a dominating tool to control partners. If you feel uncomfortable being happy when your partner is sad, they could be in control of your mood. If you rely on them to feel joy, this is not healthy.

3) You are Anxious When Separated: If you feel negative emotions when you are away from your partner, you may need to work on your spiritual fitness. Every couple should have independence and enjoy their time apart.

4) You Need Their Constant Validation: If you constantly seek praise and compliments from your partner, this can be a sign you are seeking your spiritual value from them. You need to know your worth and be comfortable with your self-assessment.

5) You Fall Apart When Relationships End: It's sad when relationships end because you have lost something you once held dear. But if relationships didn't end, then how would new one's form? If you have ever felt completely lost or bereft when a relationship ends, or you feel your life has fallen apart, then it is time to fall in love again—with yourself! Step away from seeking new relationships and focus on your spiritual life and find wholeness of mind and spirit instead.

Twin Flame Awakening Explained

One of the most frustrating parts of the twin flame process is that they don't automatically awake at the same time. This can mean that one part of the twin flame can be in stage 2 for years, waiting for their twin to evolve. If you know you are in a soul connection and are excited to meet your twin flame, you are probably the awakened twin flame while your counterpart is the sleeper twin flame.

This can lead to feelings of frustration for the awakened party as you fail to understand that they haven't felt such a strong connection and divine interaction yet. You know that you can connect to them using your higher self, and you feel their emotions in the same way, so why are they still un-awakened? This is known as the bubble love between the two souls when they can speak to each other and acknowledge each other's presence before they physically meet.

This can lead to interactions that may seem out of character. You may say something nasty or unkind to your twin via your higher self during this stage. You may be taken aback by these types of interactions and wonder why they occurred. You wouldn't say such negative things to your twin if you were face to face? Why did those thoughts and sentiments occur? Well, that's your higher self-helping you to push your twin's buttons and give them a nudge to wake up. This process is known as triggering, and although it originates from your physical being, it is an extension of your spiritual awareness. The order in which the two twins awake is generally dictated by the energy that drives them. The twin flame with feminine energy will generally be the first to wake, while the male energy is often awakened later.

10 Signs You are About to Meet Your Twin Flame

You may have spent years in the yearning state and spent the time interacting with your twin flame via your higher self. Some interactions will have been fractious, while some will have been joyful, but how do you know that a union is about to happen?

1) All Your Thoughts Are Filled with Love and Harmony: There is no negativity and sadness. Your soul knows that it is about to meet its other half, and your lower vibrations will have been cleared. You know what is coming, and you are ready for the ultimate union.

2) You are Happy and Shine with an Inner Glow: When we meet someone special, it is often apparent to others by the light that shines from within. When you're close to a meeting with your twin flame, your spiritual self can't help but radiate its joy.

3) Things in Your Life Will Change: You may feel the urge to sell your home and move to another state, district, or even country. The feeling may be confusing and make no sense to you at the time, but this is the universe sending you a message. It is guiding you to a path that will lead to your twin flame. Go with it! Do whatever feels right and let your urges dictate your future.

4) You Feel the Anticipation: If you have constant butterflies in your stomach or your skin tingles with anticipation, this is a clear sign something is going to happen. If you know about the concept of twin flames, you will recognize what is happening, but people oblivious to the concept will feel a gut feeling of anticipation without knowing why. So, if it feels like being a kid at Christmas every day, then chances are your union is about to happen. Enjoy the sensation and ready yourself for the experience.

5) All Aspects of Your Life Seem to Meet Your Expectations: One sign of a forthcoming union is the opposite of change. Your life may reach a personal zenith to prepare you for your twin flame. Your financial and professional standards are met, and you feel more comfortable and happier than you ever felt before. That promotion you wanted, the car you drive, and the people who surround you are all positive aspects of your life, and you love them dearly.

6) You Have Lost That Yearning Feeling: This is a paradoxical sign you are ready to meet your twin flame. You stop obsessing about it and communicating through your higher self. You have never felt more complete and more harmonious. You need not feel complete because you are in the best shape of your life. You may even become dismissive of the union you used to crave because you wonder why you would need another person to make you whole.

7) You Feel Inspired and Creative: This is another sign from the universe that a meeting is about to happen. You will feel inspired to write more or start an artistic project. During your period of self-improvement, you may have already dabbled with new hobbies or passions, and the universe will use them to inspire you. When you become excited and passionate about projects and missions, you become linked to your humanity and more open to messages from the spiritual realm. Once these channels are open, you need to follow your heart and get involved with the projects you feel are your destiny. They make take you away from more lucrative projects, and you may wonder what the purpose is, but you must do them! The universe doesn't send you on fools' missions, and the outcome will be worth the effort!

8) You Will be Able to Manifest Things for Yourself and Others: Some people feel manifestation is difficult and think it is an unhealthy way to gain material things. A manifestation is simple as it is a positive way of thinking, and as you connect to your spiritual self, it's used to make people around you happy. You will feel a stronger connection with the universe as your union approaches, and the ability to manifest your choices will increase.

Try these simple steps to manifest things for yourself and others:

- **Establish Your Purpose:** Tell the universe what you want and how it will affect your world. So, a manifestation isn't about telling the universe that you've always wanted a Porsche, so could you have one, please? But of course, you are connected to your spiritual side, so you know how to use your connection to the universe to benefit other people as well. If you want a raise in salary at work, then you need to explain why you want it. You can then explain who else will benefit from your financial windfall and how you will use your extra cash to make the world a better place.

- **Plan to Help Your Manifestation Work:** Now, you need to create systems to facilitate an increase in your salary. Manifestation is just a part of attainment, and you need to give it all the help you can. Create exciting new projects at work and make sure the people in charge are aware of your input. Ask for an assessment from your managers or supervisors, and be prepared to ask for your raise if the outcome is favorable. Take courses that will make you more efficient and knowledgeable to make you a candidate for a salary increase. Help your manifestation in every way you can, and you will improve your chances of realizing it.

- **Allow Manifestations to Happen:** When practicing manifestation, doubts may occur. Remember that manifestation is subject to divine timing, just like the twin flame experience, and if it is meant to happen, it will. So, allow it to happen and stay committed to your goals.

9) You Will Feel the Need to Raise Your Vibration: As the time approaches when your twin flame appears in your life, you will naturally feel the need to improve your vibration and speed your personal growth.

This can include a desire to do the following things:

- **Improve Your Diet:** You will lose any bad habits regarding food. Your inner spirit knows how you should nourish your body and will direct you to healthier options. You will already have a relatively healthy diet, but you will feel repulsed by food bad for you as twindom approaches. So, if you are overly excited by vegetables and repulsed by your favorite fast food, then this could be a sign of your impending union.

- **You Begin to Avoid Electrical Devices That Emit Blue Light:** This is a sign you are becoming more aware of your sleep and that you're working to improve sleep patterns. Why do you want better sleep patterns? So, you can interact with your twin flame in your dreams and form a stronger relationship before you meet them.

- **You Will Feel the Desire to Walk Barefoot Whenever Possible:** You will feel a natural desire to shed your footwear and embrace the earth you walk on. If you find yourself in your garden with bare feet just feeling the sensation of the grass between your toes, then your spiritual self is preparing for greater things.
- **You Will Seek Alternative Ways to Heal Your Spirit:** If you feel an overwhelming need to expand your knowledge of alternative healing, then do so. Your body and soul are telling you that you need a level of healing before you meet your twin. You may feel an affinity with reiki healers or experts who practice acupuncture or crystal healing. Go with the flow and feel the benefit of whatever form of healing available.

10) You Will Begin to Have Vivid Dreams About Your Twin: These dreams will often be the most specific signs you receive. People who have met their twin flames have described their dreams before meeting them as realistic and intense. They share the experience of meeting their twin flame in their dreams and recognizing distinct features that prove to be correct. Twins will often use the astral realm to communicate while they sleep, but they will intensify the connections once they are awake.

During their dreams, they will often hug their twin flames and whisper words of comfort and reassurance. Some people have reported their twin would embrace them and say things like "I am on my way to find you" or "trust the universe to bring us together." Keep a dream journal and write the details down every morning following your experiences because they will help you recognize your twin physically and emotionally.

Details from these dreams will help you complete all the following stages that happen after you meet. The messages you receive need to be recorded, as they will be important to both of you as your relationship grows and matures.

The bottom line is that not everyone will experience all the signs above. Some people may find their meeting is out of the blue and received no warning signs at all. Other people will find that more physical signs are a precursor to their experiences. Numerology and specific patterns can indicate the imminent arrival of your twin, so watch out for them. The main thing to remember is to let go of any fear or trepidation and stay calm. Relax and enjoy the anticipation, you can't change what is about to happen to you, but you can improve the experience. Your twin flame is going through similar emotions, and they will be just as excited and nervous. Remember, when you do meet, you may be amazed at how much you already know about each other just from your spiritual connections.

Chapter 6: Stage 3: The Maturing (Honeymoon) Phase

At last, all the signs showed that a meeting was imminent, and now they are here in your life and part of your very being. Your twin flame may have seemed like a far-off part of your life for so long you are finding it difficult to believe they're here. So, what happens now?

First, you must understand what qualities your twin flame brings to you and how they will change your life. The emotions you're feeling can be overcoming and often scary. They need to be recognized and appreciated so you can begin your twin flame mission.

When You First Meet a Twin Flame

The signs we have met a twin flame are well documented in the chapter about twin flames, so we already know what to look for. Remember, it need not be a romantic connection; it can be a friend or a mentor. They will have the same struggles with life you do, and they will display the same strengths.

You will already feel a connection with them, and you may even recognize them from your dreams. They will feel the same intense connection and may be shocked by the sense of recognition. The intensity will be unlike anything you have both experienced before, and even a look can evoke the most intense emotions imaginable.

You both know you have been brought together for a higher purpose, and this can be overwhelming. How are you meant to deal with these intense emotions and the deep and meaningful love you feel and be productive? In these early stages, it can lead to drama, chaos, and confusion.

Twin flames are connected on a higher plane, but they need to exist on earth. This means they may need to learn how to temper their relationship and adapt to more conventional forms of relationship. Even if we wanted to "regular" relationships will still be required, and it is essential to integrate your twin flame into your life.

This means they need to know how their connections differ from regular relationships and how to manage them. There are four different elements to their relationship that need to be balanced and healthy.

Discover Your Emotional Connection

The meeting of twin flames triggers the heart center's opening that allows them to love harder and deeper than ever before. Consider how a mother connects to their new baby by synchronizing their brainwaves to the baby's heartbeat, which facilitates an exchange of energy between them both. This means the mother is sensitive to the information their child is sending them, and they understand the needs and emotions their baby is experiencing.

In the same way, twin flames trigger hidden parts of each other that have been buried and unresolved in the past. Your twin flame highlights your shadow side and allows you to explore the aspects of your life that need forgiveness and understanding. Twin flames work as a team to give each other support and the courage to open their hearts and heal any wounds it may have suffered in the past.

How to Strengthen Your Neural Connections

The spiritual bond you have will already be strong, but so will the fear that your relationship won't survive such a battering of intense emotions. This can lead to anticipatory anxiety. You may both be so worried about what negative things can happen that you fail to recognize the opportunity for positivity.

Twin flames already feel they mirror each other, but how can that sensation be strengthened? Much like more traditional partnerships, the honeymoon period is often a time for discovering what your other half is all about.

> **1) Study Your Partner:** Your spiritual bonds may be unbreakable, but what are the more practical parts of your life you share? Remember, at some point, the two of you are destined to achieve greatness and the passions you share may be the key to discovering your destiny. Ask them about the joys and highlights of their life before you met and why they love what they do. What books do they love? What are their favorite foods and places to visit? You know you are special, but you still need to put the work into getting to know your partner.
>
> **2) Develop Trust:** You must never lie to your partner and make sure you are always there for them. Be honest about your feelings, even when confusing and bewildering. Your twin flame should be the person you turn to in times of trouble, but they can also be the reason you are in turmoil! You need to communicate every emotion and trust them to be there for you.

3) Fight Fair: Even in this fairytale period, you will have issues with your partner, and it's tempting to use harsh words and accusations to get your point across. This can be damaging to both parties and can leave deep scars.

Try these simple rules when you disagree:

- **Know Exactly What You Are Arguing About:** Are you *really* having a full-on fight about dirty clothes on the bathroom floor, or is it just a handy reason to cause an argument? Sometimes partners will use petty excuses to cause trouble because they have underlying issues. Make sure your discussions are centered on real reasons and not just manufactured ones.

- **Avoid Absolutes:** It is much more dramatic to use phrases like "you never pick your clothes up" when the truth is saying, "I wish you would be tidier and pick up your dirty clothes," is more diplomatic. Avoid putting your partner in defensive mode and shutting down the argument.

- **Take Breaks:** If you are feeling emotionally battered, then ask for a time out. Acknowledge that the disagreement isn't resolved, and you know you still need to talk but give yourself a break. Take twenty minutes to walk off your intense emotions and return calmer and more reasonable. This can also give your partner time to regroup and see things clearer.

- **Honor Each Other's Boundaries**: Don't take cheap shots you know will leave a mark. You may feel victorious for about a second, but afterward, you will regret causing your twin flame pain. Above all others, you know the wounds they carry and the areas of their life that are sensitive, and how to land the most damaging blows. Be a better person and avoid cheap shots as they will only make your partner lose trust in you.

- **Extend the Olive Branch:** Know when you have both reached your limits and allow your partner to end the argument with dignity. Make a joke or reach out to hold their hand. All arguments should finish with a mutual recovery point. You've both said what was needed, so move on and recover the closeness you have.

How to Strengthen Your Physical Connection

When you meet your twin flame, remarkable changes occur to your physical self and your spiritual being. The meeting of your twin souls will release a form of energy known as Kundalini. This energy will fill you both with such euphoria; you will feel the need to hug and kiss people while embracing life with a glorious feeling of energy. Though, it can also lead to physical symptoms that can be confusing to both parties.

Below we will consider spiritual and physical symptoms when light and dark forms are released. This doesn't mean that the energy is good or bad. It is simply a form of energy that exists within us and is released when we meet our twin flames.

Light Awakening Symptoms

- You lose all sense of ego and feel a connected with the higher plane that is more intense than ever before.
- You feel blessed and bathed in love.
- You become at one with the world and feel intense compassion for humanity.

- You feel intense pleasure at the simplest things.
- There are no limits on your ambitions; you feel inspired to achieve greatness.
- You experience amazing synchronicity with those people you love.
- A veil is lifted on your past behaviors, and you understand the impact you have had on others.
- You can see how your mind works and picture the physical journey of your thoughts.
- The universe blesses you with "downloads" of information that allow you to become more enlightened.

Dark Awakening Symptoms

- You can experience quite violent convulsions and alarming periods of shaking.
- You become extra sensitive to external stimuli, the TV sounds too loud, the lights are too bright, and you need to escape and be alone.
- You experience disturbed periods of sleep.
- You experience your self-identity transcending your body, and the lack of ego means it no longer affects your life.
- There can be periods of intense hallucinations when you struggle to distinguish what is real from what is imagined. This can lead to you feeling like you're going crazy.
- Feelings of impending doom that will dominate you for a short period until they are dispelled by the feeling of gentle energy that melts them away until they vanish.

These symptoms are quite common and can be terrifying, but they won't happen to everyone. Spiritual energy connections are individual experiences, but when you meet your twin flame, you have the added bonus of shared experiences to make you stronger.

Some people have reported that when they meet their mirror soul, they are immediately attracted to them sexually, while others report a loss in libido. This can indicate the sort of relationship you are destined to have with your twin flame. For instance, it wouldn't be appropriate to have a burning desire to rip your mentors' clothes off when you first meet them!

Less Common Awakening Symptoms:

- Exhaustion with no obvious cause can happen, and you may feel shattered and lack a spiritual center in the early stages.
- Dreams about serpents and snakes are sometimes present. Kundalini energy is often called the serpent energy.
- Feeling stripped of emotions and feelings defenseless like a newborn child is a symptom of your rebirth as a spiritual being and can feel terrifying.
- Highs and lows of energy levels with no obvious reason are other less common ones.
- Hallucinating sounds, and hearing music nobody else can hear can occur.
- You experience flashbacks to your former lives and recognize other people's past life experiences, especially if they affected yours.
- You are overwhelmed by sadness at the state of mankind, and you feel a need to repair the planet with your twin flame.
- You have out-of-body experiences when you transcend the earth and connect to your higher self.

- You experience food cravings and aversions just like a pregnant female does.
- You have intense orgasms even without physical contact.
- Undiagnosable physical symptoms like intense headaches, nausea, skin breakouts, and digestive issues can be symptoms of awakening.

This release of energy can be a joyous time for both of you, providing you are prepared for it. Be there to support each other and take care of yourself and your nervous system.

Become the compassionate crutch you both need and take care of each other. You are in the honeymoon phase, and this can sound like a perfect time, but it all depends on how you react to the barrage of new experiences you are undergoing.

How to Get the Most from the Honeymoon Period

Just because you are twin flames, it doesn't mean you are somehow exempt from "normal" ways of honeymooning. This can be part of a romantic couple's timeline, or it could be two friends finding themselves on vacation. Taking a break from the relentless noise and stress of everyday life will help you both feel in a better place about your relationship. If you have a healthy budget, then the world is filled with dream destinations you can both explore, so let's consider some idyllic destinations where you can honeymoon in style.

Spiritual Honeymoon Spots

1) Omega Institute for Holistic Studies: Nestled in the picturesque Hudson Valley, this retreat offers seasonal activities to appeal to everyone. In summer, you can travel to New York and join like-minded people doing a variety of events. You can canoe, swim or kayak on the lake or try walking the onsite labyrinth. There are classes in meditation, yoga, and other spiritual practices, or you can take advantage of the impressive 7,000-volume library to work on your creative journey. Visitors are encouraged to tailor their stay to suit their needs, and the staff will work with you to ensure your trip is everything you want and need.

2) Miraval: In the depths of southern Arizona, you can find this amazing top spa resort, ranked as one of the best in the U.S. While it may look like a traditional spa resort with all the luxury and comfort that entails, look closely at the packages they provide.

Miraval provides a unique experience called the Equine experience. They encourage visitors to let go of their fears and self-doubt by interacting with specially trained horses. They also have programs that deal with sexual aspects of life that can help you both work through any intimacy issues.

3) Canyon Reach: With resorts in four different parts of the U.S., the Canyon Ranch ethos is to help you achieve health and wellbeing. They offer balanced gourmet meals alongside nutritional classes to help you understand how food governs your overall health. They provide a medical check service to make sure guests have the right level of fitness to participate in their programs. This upscale retreat is the ultimate way to get fit and benefit from their professional services while still having the perfect honeymoon.

4) Shreyas Yoga Retreat Bangalore: This Indian ashram offers a spiritual paradise in one of the most beautiful parts of the continent for the more adventurous travelers. There are just twelve rooms set in 25 acres of garden, so every guest has a unique experience and is treated as part of the family. This resort differs from most spa-type holidays as it focuses on taking the guests on a spiritual journey. This includes more traditional yoga and spa treatments, but it is also about interacting with nature.

The guests are encouraged to participate in nature-based activities in the area and to visit local villages. They are given a chance to see how local children work in the surrounding fields, and they can help prepare meals at a local orphanage. This type of experience is guaranteed to promote soul searching and a degree of humility.

5) **Turtle Island Fiji:** This resort is more suited to romantic couples, but it can be booked as friends. There are never over 14 couples at the resort at any time, so you will never feel crowded or overwhelmed. Each couple has a private beach and can get married in a traditional Fijian ceremony that includes traditional attire and a wedding raft. Meals are served in a communal outdoor setting and served with the finest French champagne available. While this may seem rather luxurious and less spiritual, the setting is perfect for you to get to know your twin flame better.

Not everyone can abandon real life and travel to far-flung destinations to explore their relationships, so how are you meant to connect when other people keep interrupting? Share your favorite things. This can be as simple as renting a film (old style) and watching it with a pizza and wine.

Your mirror soul is just as excited as you are about the experience you are going through so take advantage of this. Snatch a weekend to go camping together and commune with nature together. Watching a sunset with the person you have been dreaming about for your whole life can be just as intense as visiting any retreat. Feeling the sensation of warm rain on your face can fill your soul with joy that is as satisfying as sex. Your connection is real, but it will also be subject to trauma, so remember to have fun as you enjoy the intensity of your mirror self.

Chapter 7: Stage 4: The Testing (Crisis Phase)

When does the testing phase begin? This can differ depending on the relationship and the level of contact the twin flames have with each other. If you are living with your twin flame, then the testing phase probably will happen sooner. If you only see your twin flame at work or socially, then you may go for years before you reach this stage.

Most couples will begin to experience changes in their relationship following their first serious disagreement. We all know that even the healthiest relationship will suffer setbacks, but why are twin flames more affected by turmoil and problems in their relationship? The truth is because their relationship has ascended from a more regular 3D dimension to a higher plane, everything is elevated, and every emotion is heightened.

The Main Causes of Turmoil in the Crisis Phase

Once doubts have set in it can open the floodgates for more negative emotions about your relationships. You have spent your honeymoon period believing you are bulletproof. Together you exist in a fairytale, and every day you notice new similarities between you and your twin. You have the perfect relationship, and nothing can break you...until it does!

Why Does Distancing Occur Between People Who are So Connected?

Consider the facts. A "regular" relationship is between two people who feel attraction or kindred feelings between two individuals who can be quite different. Their personalities are contrasting, and their interests may be poles apart. They develop their relationship by trying different things and discovering if they can co-exist even though they are so atypical. That's the joy of regular relationships and finding out if other people can live with your quirks and foibles.

Twin flames are different. They are two halves of the same being, so they should never clash, right? Well, consider how you existed before you met your mirror image. Did you find every aspect of yourself perfect? Were you filled with self-confidence and never felt the need for self-improvement? Many people don't have those levels of self-worth, and this can be the root cause of turmoil in the relationship.

After all, it is a lot easier to love someone who is different from you and completes you as a couple. Still, if you don't love yourself as you are, then how can you love a mirror image of yourself?

If you are in an intimate relationship with your twin, then sex can be the trigger to your period of turmoil. The act of intimacy will trigger past wounds and traumas. You will both question if the accumulated negativity you bring to the relationship can be overcome. An overload of information can lead to a sense of drama, becoming the main focus of your connection.

Why is Drama So Addictive?

The emotional triggers from both of your pasts can create a whirlwind of turmoil that means you cease to function in positive ways. You become too focused on the heartbreak and trauma from past experiences you are both stuck within the moment and will fail to find the energy to move forward.

Once the body experiences drama, the brain will release chemicals like those found in opiates. This means that as the drama escalates, the more the body craves it. Some people believe that love and attention only happen when they create a situation based on tension. They feel that testing the people who love them is the only way they will be sure they will stay no matter what happens.

Like other addictions, as the body and mind develop a tolerance, the level of drama needs to increase. For twin flames, this is even more apparent. They are the mirror halves of each other, and so, if one of them is addicted to drama, then they both are! As a couple, they will dredge up matters from the past to illustrate why they are so afraid of being hurt. They will be more focused on problems they can lose sight of the positive mission they should be focusing on.

Here is How to Tell if You Are Stuck in Twin Flame Drama:

1) **You Are Always Telling the World About Your Relationship:** If you find yourself on social media changing your relationship status and posting on forums and blogs about your personal life, then you could be addicted to your own drama!

2) Your Mind Replays Your Times of Conflict: Even when you aren't with your twin, or you have given each other a break, you just can't let it go. Your mind is buzzing with the conversations and disagreements the two of you have had. This automatic analysis means you're constantly questioning yourself and your relationships with each other and other people. You will be overwhelmed by the fears and anger filling your head, and you will constantly worry about the past and the future.

3) You Have Arguments with Yourself: In your mind, you are persistently arguing with yourself about how the relationship is going. You play Devil's advocate for your twin and becoming angry with yourself and them.

4) Your Former Identity Has Faded into the Past: When you think about yourself, you do so as a unit. You identify as part of your twin flame rather than as an individual. Deep down, you know that your individuality is becoming a thing of the past, and it has gone missing since you met your flame.

5) You Justify Your Negative Experiences and Compare Them with Other Twin Flame Stories: If you search for examples of unhappy twin unions and comparing them to yours, then you may be focusing on the wrong part of your relationship!

6) You Relentlessly Turn to Other People for Advice: If you can't go more than a couple of days without checking the Internet for spiritual advice or consulting a tarot card reader, you may be in trouble. Insight into your situation should be based on your relationship and not on some "oracle" or psychic expert.

7) Your Drama is the Main Subject of Conversation: Have you noticed people rolling their eyes or making excuses to leave whenever you talk about your twin flame and the problems you are having? This is a sure sign you have let your relationship and the drama it creates take over your life. What about your other passions and interests?

How to End the Circle of Drama and Focus on the Positive Aspects of Your Relationship

1) Check Out for a Moment: Step back, take yourself out of the situation, and catch your breath. Sit in a dark room and focus on your breathing while telling yourself that something needs to change. You know you are spiraling out of control, and it's time to get back to a form of normality.

2) Clear Your Energy: When you are in the crisis stage, you are filled with dark energy that governs your life. You're addicted to your drama, and it can feel like a track of music constantly playing on a loop inside your brain. Drama can get stuck in your psyche and follow you into your dreams. The best way to clear these feelings is to remove any negative energy and start with a clean slate.

Try these effective yet simple energy-cleansing methods.

- **Cut the Cord:** Who is the main protagonist when it comes to your drama? Your twin is, of course. But who else is on the edge of your relationship putting their nose into your business? Picture all the people causing you turmoil, and mentally let them go. Think of them and visualize a cord that attaches them to you. Now say, "I bless you with positive energy, and I let you go" as you cut the cord. Watch as they drift away and feel the space this leaves in your spiritual space. Each night as you go to sleep, consider what attachments you have formed that day and let them go. This helps you sleep better with a clear mind and a healthy mental attitude.

- **Clear Negative Thoughts:** Take a notebook and write down any negativity you have encountered recently. When twin flames found a union, they can trigger some pretty devastating past emotions. These can result from decades of repressed feelings and can overwhelm your state of balance. Some of these thought-forms originate from personal experiences, or they can be as random as the opinion and expectation of others. Maybe you think you aren't good enough for your twin, or they deserve better. This is a harmful way to think, and you need to dispel any negative, redundant, and repetitive thought forms to make way for positive thoughts. Picture a bright white cleansing light to help eliminate any spiritual debris invading your energy field.

- **Create a Sacred Space:** If the emotional battles between yourself and your twin are inevitable, then you need a place to recharge. Your energy is like a battery, and recharging is essential. This type of space can be a physical space like a quiet room in your house or the local park. A trip to the beach or other local beauty spots will help you regroup and raise your positivity. If physical options aren't available, then create an energizing space in your mind. Picture yourself in space or on another planet to get the most from your visualization.

- **Have a Good Cry:** Have you ever wondered why children cry so often? They recognize that crying is an emotional release that also cleanses their energy and causes positive vibrations. As adults, we are conditioned to keep our crying to a minimum and put on a brave face when faced with trauma. Let it out. If you feel emotionally drained, you need to clean your aura, and crying will do that. You may feel unable to let go of your repression and seek a trigger to start you crying. So, put a suitably sad film on your iPad and grab a handful of tissues and let it all out!

- **Take a Salt Bath:** To clean your energy and your body, then this traditional type of relaxation is perfect. Salt is one of the most natural cleansing elements, and sea salt is even more effective. Use Himalayan, Epsom, or regular sea salt in a hot bath to draw out all the negative energy you are holding on to.

3) Let Go of Attachments to Groups or Online Connections That Involve Twin Flames: Your experience with your twin should be between the two of you. Yes, it's informative to channel into other people's experiences and get embroiled in their trauma and conflicts, but it can also mess with your mind. You can create strife without knowing it just by bringing other people's drama into your relationship. Detach yourself from outside influences, and you will have the chance to identify what is within your union that is causing conflict.

4) Forgive and Forget: Once your energy is cleansed, then it's time to build some bridges. Contact your twin and ask them to forgive you because you forgive them. This can help you start again and build into the couple you know you can be. You both need to be in a good place for this to happen, or you will end up back on the hamster wheel of emotions you are looking to get off. Remember that essentially, you are truly one and the same. Any drama and turmoil won't benefit either of you. In fact, it damages both of you and it needs to be addressed. If you feel your twin has deliberately hurt, you then consider what that says about their emotional state. Nobody hurts other people when they are in a place of joy. Hurt comes from hurt and possible fear of what is happening to you both.

5) Replace Your Addiction to Drama with Another Positive Activity: Even when you are determined to expel drama from your relationship, you must realize that you are both going to miss it and the part it played in your union. Fill this void with another healthy activity, so you can both move forward with a new pattern to replace the old one. Consider the part that chewing gum can play for people who are trying to give up smoking. Many former smokers will tell you that gum is more effective than anything else when trying to kick the habit because it gets rid of a negative habit by replacing it with a new one. Exercise, cooking, reading a book, or catching up with Netflix will all work. Eating a piece of fruit or listening to new music will also provide you with something else to "chew" on.

6) Repeat When Necessary: The methods explained above are not a one size fits all solution for twin flame relationships, but they will help. You may need to practice them every day, but only the two of you will know your relationship's true status. All connections require work to endure over time, and you have spent so long anticipating your romantic twin flame arriving that it would be tragic to let drama spoil it.

How Non-Romantic Twin Flame Relationships Create Turmoil

Surely, when you connect with your twin flame in a way that doesn't involve intimacy or sex, you remove all the tension that romantic ties create, don't you? That is what we would like to believe, but anybody who has experienced the relationship between soul mates and ultimately twin flames knows otherwise.

Once you have connected to your soul group or your mirror soul, you have experienced a dimensional shift that transcends most human experiences. You are likely a spiritually healthy being to experience these types of connections, which can make you dismissive of other people who aren't as developed as you are. Even when you are becoming the better spiritual version of yourself, you are raising the bar. You are physically better and emotionally stronger, and you find it difficult to understand how other people aren't putting in the same effort.

This shift of perception can throw your world into chaos even before you meet your twin flame so imagine how the pair of you will react. Knowing what may happen to your individual and joint relationships will help you to prepare yourself for the inevitable conflict that will occur.

1) You Will Lose Friends: You are changing as a person, and the energy your twin flame connection brings will elevate you into a higher place. This will disconnect you from people who were in your life before you ascended, and they may feel uncomfortable in your presence. Your vibrational frequencies will clash, and they will feel cut off and abandoned. Some of the most influential people in your life, even those you have known from childhood, will fall away, but don't worry because you are now part of a different club. Tap into the worldwide twin flame experience and mix with people who understand the concept of twin flame experiences.

2) You Will Change Jobs: The shift of dimensions will affect all aspects of your life. Fact. You will begin to expect better things whenever and wherever you are. Consider it your V.I.P. status shift when you move from coach to first class. Your soul will want more, and it will push you out of your comfort zone to achieve what it believes is your destiny. You may blame your twin flame for these uncomfortable feelings and wishing you had never met them. This is just a phase on the road to your joint mission to success. There will be periods of unrest but hang in there because the outcome will justify the difficult times.

3) You May Lose Contact with Family Members: When your twin flame is not part of your more traditional circle, then it can cause conflict. Your family expects you to be focused on them and their needs and wants, so it can be disruptive when that focus shifts. As you change and expect better things, they can remain stagnant and uninvolved in your present activities, and that's fine. Families are all about drama and intrigue, so it can be inevitable that problems occur. Cut out toxic connections and concentrate on your spiritual health. Remember, just because you were born into a group of people doesn't mean you are tied to them for life.

4) You Will Become Intolerant of Petty Actions: You and your twin are filled with higher vibrations that let you live your true life without focusing on lower-level activities. The problem is that mere humans tend to indulge in these lower-level behaviors, and it will become repugnant to you. Gossips, bullies, liars, cheats, and fearmongers will all be discarded. The old you may have allowed for their behavior, but the newly enlightened you will lead a better life. You won't necessarily look down on them or pity their existence;

you will just choose not to engage with them. Your twin flame may be blamed for your new attitude, and this may cause conflict.

5) Alcohol and Other Stimulants Are No Longer Part of Your Life: Once you have experienced the highs of twin flame connectivity, then there is no substitute. You understand what drives you, and it isn't the standard toxins on which other humans rely. Higher vibrational frequencies lead to a spontaneous natural cleaning of the system. You will become more affected by natural stimulants and, as such, won't need to turn to caffeine or sugar to raise your energy levels. This can lead to conflict amongst your social group since you no longer need to visit bars or coffee shops, and you prefer to feed your soul with trips to museums and culturally enriching venues.

6) You Will Follow Your Soul Rather Than Your Ego: You will understand the importance of the divine plan and how it governs your life. Once you let go of the traditional belief that your ego is running the show, you become more instantaneous and willing to go with the flow. This can cause conflict if your divine plan goes against other people's needs and wants in your life.

It's important to understand is that all twin flame relationships go through the conflict stage. Some will survive and go on to thrive; others will take a different path.

Chapter 8: Stage 5: The Chasing or Running

At this stage of the relationship, you may both be exhausted by all the turmoil and turbulence you have been through. All those years of yearning for "the one" and wishing you could feel complete seem to be firmly in the past. Those heady days of attraction and love have been obliterated by the stress and anxiety caused by your crisis stage.

Chances are your souls are at different levels of maturity, and one of you will find the intensity more difficult to handle. The younger soul will often feel the need to escape, while the older soul will become the partner called *the chaser*. Most twin flame couples will experience this stage, but their length will vary greatly depending on personalities and circumstances.

If you become the chaser in your relationship, it's important to understand what to look for as your partner begins to run. Knowing the signs can prepare you for their departure and help you understand why the relationship needs to take a break. There should be no recriminations about separating; it could be the healthiest thing you can do as a couple, but the role you both play should be determined before you begin this stage of the twin flame journey.

How to Recognize if Your Twin Flame is a Runner

First, you need to understand that the grand prize in a twin flame relationship is not always a lifelong romantic involvement. The male divine soul will often feel the need to have other relationships, despite connecting with their female divine soul. That's just how the masculine soul works, and there is no use trying to understand why this happens.

Runners don't always know why they leave; they just feel that separation from their twin is the only way to progress. This doesn't mean the feelings they have are less intense than the chaser, they are just less equipped to deal with them. The process will begin when the runner begins to doubt the connection is what they want, and they will begin to pull away in different ways.

1) Ghosting: This is possibly one of the cruelest ways of withdrawing from a relationship. It means the runner will suddenly, without warning, withdraw all forms of communication and fail to respond to any of your messages. Your first reaction will be to wonder what has happened, maybe they have been hurt or a family emergency has caused them to leave town. Upon closer inspection, you realize that they have cut you out of their life. You are blocked on social media; they have changed their number, and you have no other way of communicating with them.

Why would anybody choose such a brutal way to end things? If you consider it from the runner's perspective, it is a quick and easy way out. There is no drama, hysterics, difficult conversations, or explanations needed. They simply leave, and you are left to deal with the mess.

2) They Bench You: This is a method used by twins who are eager to keep all their options open. They will give you the love you need one day and then treat you like a random acquaintance the next day. They aren't willing to completely close the door, but they still want to see what else is out there. This doesn't always mean withdrawing sexual contact, as this is more of a 3-dimensional reaction to benching. With twin flames, the relationship will often transcend sex, and the runner will blow hot and cold about deeper relationship aspects. They will tell you their most intimate feelings and then treat you like a stranger.

3) They Get Involved with Groups of People Who are Not in Your Social Circle: When your twin spends more time with their friends or colleagues, they are trying to exclude you from their life. Don't be insulted, but be prepared that they may be leaving the relationship.

4) Withdraw Commitment Levels: Because of the nature of your relationship, there may be social taboos that cause society to frown on your union. While you may feel you can both get past these obstacles, they may be less convinced.

Here are some of the most common obstacles to twin flame relationships:

- **Age Gaps:** Your twin flame may be a lot younger than you, and your relationship could raise eyebrows.

- **Unethical Relationships:** If your twin is held back by convention, they may feel the need to run. Some examples are a lawyer/client, student/teacher, doctor/patient, etc. You may be willing to make the changes needed for the relationship to work, but they aren't.

- **Different Sexual Orientation:** One of you may be naturally gay while the other is heterosexual.
- **Current Relationships:** When you form your relationship, you may already be in loving partnerships with other people. Some twins will find it hard to abandon these partnerships and choose to be loyal rather than follow their hearts.
- **Distance:** Although your divine plan will give you nudges to take you to your twin, you may end up living on different continents! It may be easier for your twin to adapt to their physical surroundings rather than move and uproot their lives.
- **Cultural Differences:** Culture hugely influences some people, and your twin may feel uncomfortable shedding the beliefs and behaviors they have been brought up with.

How Can You Repair Your Relationship?

Within your union, you are aware that you need help to resolve your issues. Your partner has upset you, and you have upset them. The type of love you both feel for each other affects you and is overwhelming. The following exercise is an effective way to place your cards on the table and have a full and frank discussion with your partner and yourself.

The Mirroring Exercise:

1) Make time to sit in a quiet place with a piece of paper and a pen.

2) Now is the chance for you to put your issues down in black and white. Use short sentences to record your thoughts and emotions. Use sentences like "I am upset with my twin flame because he uses harsh words to get a reaction

from me" or "I dislike my twin flame when he pressures me to spend time with him."

3) Now, rewrite the statements with different pronouns to make them about yourself. For instance, "I am upset with myself because I use harsh words to get a reaction from my twin."

4) Are there any truths in the sentences you have just written? Sometimes the issues we have with others originate with ourselves. Are you misinterpreting things because you know you have negative reactions to certain situations? Are you pressuring your partner because you need to pressure yourself?

5) Imagine your inner pain and hurt as a separate physical part of you and have a conversation with it. Ask it what it needs to feel better and heal. Hug it and spend time with it until it feels healed. Only then can you let it reintegrate with yourself and become whole once more.

This exercise will help you have more controlled conversations with your twin and listen to what they are trying to tell you. Mirroring is a potent way to talk to your inner turmoil and should be practiced whenever needed.

Defining of the Runner/Chaser Phase

When one half of the couple becomes scared of the connection, physical distancing doesn't always reflect it. They may lack the courage to leave the relationship, but they will become more distant.

Signs your twin is the runner even though they are physically staying put.

- **They Turn to Distractions Like Drugs and Other Stimulants:** Most people in twin flame relationships need not rely on external stimuli. Clean energy brings them all the pleasure they need, so when one twin turns to artificial forms of pleasure, they are looking to break free. Alcohol and drugs are the most common ways to find a release from the intensity they are feeling. They will do anything to block out the barrage of emotions that your partnership is subject to.
- **They Find Excuses Not to be Alone with You:** Do you find you are both spending less time alone? Does your partner surround the two of you with other people and grow anxious if the number of people dwindles? This can mean they need a break from the intensity that happens when there are no distractions. Let them organize your social life this way if you are comfortable with it. This may be all they need to convince them to stay. If you challenge them, it can make them bolt.
- **They are Overwhelmed When They are with You:** Less mature souls can feel anxious and stressed when faced with their mirror soul. They will display irritability when alone with their partner and try to cause disagreements as an excuse to leave. Mood swings are inevitable as they don't understand why they are experiencing such high levels of stress; after all, isn't this relationship the pinnacle of all unions?

Unlike regular relationships, your twin flame won't signal their unhappiness with physical or mental abuse. There is no excuse for this behavior in any partnership. Your twin flame shouldn't cheat on you either; they know the true depth of your love and would never hurt you or cheat. If you do experience this behavior, it probably isn't your twin flame.

Remember, the running phase is probably triggered by their lack of spiritual maturity. They may not have been fully prepared for your union, and they need to work on themself before you can form a successful partnership. If so, the best thing you can do for them is to give them your blessing and tell them you will always be there for them if they want to return.

Will Your Twin Flame Return?

Here's the kicker: Twin flames that run away will often come back, sometimes more than once. You may be entering a phase of your union filled with separations and reunions. No one knows what will happen, but they will return if they are your true twin flame. The term *chaser* can be misleading. After all, you shouldn't physically chase them because *they decide when* to return.

Consider Why They Ran Away

When one person is left behind in a relationship, it can be lonely, but it can also be rewarding if you use the time wisely. Take the time to consider these points:

- Are you sure they are your true twin flame and not just part of your soul group?
- Do you feel you still have things you need to accomplish together? Or do you feel that your relationship has reached a natural end?
- You may have unprepared for the meeting, and you need to do more work on your personal growth.
- You are not destined to spend the rest of your life chasing them; the decision is yours to make.

How to Chase a Runner

First, don't panic. Relax and form a plan. You still have your life to lead and other relationships to maintain. It is unhealthy to put all your energies into one channel, and you still need to look after yourself, and your spiritual health. So, stop worrying about what might happen and concentrate on the here and now. Your twin flame relationship differs from anything you have experienced on the spiritual plane, so you have no point of reference. Avoid looking at other people's experiences, and instead, choose the best way to convince your partner to return.

You might be the more spiritually mature one in your twin flame connection, but that doesn't mean you need not work on yourself.

1) **Raise Your Personal Vibrations:** Remember when you were in the yearning stage? You knew a meeting was possible, and you wanted to be in the best spiritual shape when it happened. Have you neglected your vibrations during your time together? Have you been too focused on your twin to give yourself some love? Take the time to raise your vibration and let your twin flame know you are still there for them, no matter how far away they are.

Tips on how to raise your vibration and send love to your twin flame:

- **Be Grateful for the Time You Had Together:** It's impossible to feel anger and fear when filled with gratitude. Every time you feel low energy threatening to overwhelm, try remembering what you are grateful for. This is a great way to ramp up your vibes!

- **Visualize the Love You Feel for Them:** Imagine they are with you, and you are sharing the connection you have formed. Love is one of the highest vibrating states of being, and your twin can pick up your vibrations wherever they are.

- **Be Generous:** Are you feeling lonely without your twin? Smile at a stranger. If you are generous with the love you give, you will receive the same love, if not more, in return. When you give your time, money, and love freely, you raise your spiritual vibe.

- **Forgive:** Are you feeling resentful toward your twin? Do you blame them for leaving you alone? Consider their feelings. Would you come back to a partner who feels hostile toward you? Forgive them for all that has happened, and you increase the chances of them returning.

- **Choose High Vibe Entertainment:** Everyone knows the benefit of high fiber food and high-energy ingredients, but you are affected by everything you consume. Do your entertainment choices leave you uplifted or depleted? Fill your time with content that makes you happy and energized rather than sad and anxious. Are all your social media sources healthy, or do some leave you feeling insecure? Consider changing your settings to increase your vibrations by limiting your time online and communing with nature instead. Change your music choices and discover new genres you may love.

- **Make Sure Your Relationship Vibes are Buzzing:** If you have been too busy focusing on your twin, some of your other connections may have suffered. Get back in touch with people and surround yourself with people who make you feel good. It can be too easy to sit around moping the loss of your twin and to lower your frequency, but how will that help you guide them back to you? When you have healthy relationships with others, you are signaling you are ready to try again.

2) Remain Open to the Signs: Remember back in the yearning stage when you were aware of the twin flame's signs? When you are the chaser, the universe will once more step in and guide you toward reunion if it feels you are ready. If you see repeated adverts to visit a resort or another country that seem to fit perfectly with your timeline, then do it. Pay attention to the messages the universe is sending you, and you may find yourself in the right place at the right time! Of course, the universe could just be telling you that you need a break following your recent turmoil!

3) Talk to Them Through the Higher Plane: You may have found it challenging to communicate your true feelings when you were together physically. Your own emotions and perspectives may have muddied the waters for communicating clearly. Now you are physically separated, it is easier to consider their side of any conflicts. They may be the mirror part of your soul, but you are both influenced by the experiences that happened before you met. You're different genetically and can have different personalities depending on the environment you were brought up in. Empathize with them and have conversations rather than arguments.

Should You End the Relationship Forever?

If your relationship has been the best experience ever despite the contradictions, conflict, and turmoil you endured, then, of course, you want to reunite. Yet, most twin flame relationships are destined to be temporary as the work needed to maintain them can be exhausting. If you can ride the waves of emotions and reach a tranquil shore, then you might both stay together forever, but sometimes it must end.

Here are signs that it is time to stop running or chasing:

1) You stop regarding your relationship as a safe place to be. You stop thinking of your twin as your "home" as the trauma of your union has taken over.

2) You are cold and dismissive of each other. If you contact your twin and they are rude and disdainful to you, it could be time to call it a day. When chasing your twin, they should still treat you with respect, if not love. Twin flames aren't meant to be enemies. Ever.

3) You feel that chasing or running is a waste of time. If you lose interest in any part of the process, then the relationship has run its course. Have the conversation and end it properly. Your twin needs to know exactly where they stand as they may have expectations for the future. You love each other even if you can't maintain a partnership. Do the right thing and end it cleanly.

4) Your gut tells you to end it. It is as simple as that. You have trusted your instinct and the universe to guide you in the past, so if it tells you to let go, then listen!

5) You know you will only heal once the process is complete. Sometimes the wounds you have endured are too deep and any further communications will only cause pain, and you aren't willing to take that path.

What to Take Away from a Twin Flame Relationship

First, realize that this relationship is unlike any other. You may have ended it and gone your separate ways, but you will still be part of your twin no matter what. When you part, it is normal to go through the traditional feelings of grief, anger, and hatred, followed by acceptance and forgiveness. Embrace all these emotions and use them to assimilate the lessons you have learned.

You need to celebrate the good times and let go of the bad experiences. This is the way your soul develops and steps closer to your spiritual transformation. Your twin flame relationship will stay with you, and while it may have ended in this reality, you will meet again!

Chapter 9: Stage 6: The Surrendering

This stage of the twin flame journey has been described as the magic formula or silver bullet of the process. You need to give up the final vestiges of power you have over your destiny. You reach a point when you understand that being powerless is possibly the most powerful way to live. The key is to realize what you have and let go of the attachment you may have to things and people you may think you need, but you know you can't have.

You need to believe that the universe has your destiny covered. You need to lose the fear that the relationship with your twin is based on your ego and actions. Surrender yourself to the divine and let go of the residual parts of the experience you still feel you control. Imagine your union as a rose. You have been happy to give the petals to the universe, yet you have hung on to the thorns. You are unwilling to let go of your partnership's shadowy areas, and you still cling to the sore points and moral challenges because your ego is telling you they are shameful.

Surrendering is all about realizing that you don't get to choose what parts of your love you show to the world. This depiction of your relationship needs to be whole before you can understand how it works. Roses wouldn't exist with just petals; the thorns need to be included as essential parts of the whole flower.

You need to open your mind and body to the love you have with your twin flame and let it ascend earthly boundaries. Your ego is a lust-filled part of you that seeks judgment and thrives on the boundaries society puts in place. But why should you be held back by such material boundaries? The whole point of a twin flame relationship is to transcend the barriers that exist when it comes to love. You need to accept that your love will not be restricted or imprisoned by differences and conformities. You will allow yourself to love unconditionally no matter what the obstacles in place.

A Higher Love

Surrendering to your flame means you are walking away from society's paradigms and becoming part of a more spiritual way of loving. So, what if your twin flame is from a different culture or religion to you? Are they in a relationship with someone else? Guess what? Relationships end all the time. If they want to be with you, it will happen. Parents that stay together for the sake of children is an old-fashioned concept that rarely works out well. Surrendering is all about putting yourself first and allowing your needs to be met. Every time you put yourself last, you are putting everybody else last as well.

Are you ready to be brave and refuse to waste another lifetime ruled by fear? Break away from traditional ties and face the world with a confident belief in yourself. Let yourself heed the call of the exquisite yet illogical form of love because it is meant to be. No matter what the barriers society places before you break them down and live the life ruled by destiny. The universe won't give up on you, and it will follow you until you become emancipated and embrace your twin flame experience with every fiber of your being.

What to Expect When You Surrender

When your ego governs you, you believe that inner peace is only possible when the world is aligned, and everything is perfect. When you surrender, you embrace the notion that only when you feel at peace will everything fall into place. So basically, you are turning your world upside down and changing your belief system.

You will also learn of the many realizations that will help you accept your fate.

1) **You Will Focus Less on Your Twin Flame Relationship and Begin to Focus on Yourself.**

2) **The Connection You Have with Your Twin Will be Filled with Happiness:** You now know that every negative emotion you project will radiate back and cause you harm because you are a mirror image of each other.

3) **The Only Part of Your Twin Flame Connection You are in Control of is Your Own:** You can't control how they think or react.

4) **In the Past, You Have Been Drawn to Emotionally Harmful Relationships, and You Felt They Were Your Destiny:** That is why you were constantly looking for flaws in the union with your twin flame.

5) **You Will Lose the Need for More Fulfillment:** You become appreciative of what you have and become grateful for every moment.

6) **You Will Be More Comfortable Alone:** You don't need other people to complete you because you are filled with positive energy.

7) **Communication with Your Twin Flame Will Be More Vivid:** Once you accept that the universe is responsible for your fate as a couple, then you will use other means to be together. Use the astral plane to spend time with your

partner and talk to them. Share a cuddle or just lie together in harmony. These connections will be just as real as physical interactions.

8) You Will Find Yourself Sending Love to Your Twin Regularly: Telling them you love them will encourage them to respond when they feel ready.

9) You Will Slow Down: Modern life is hectic, and it can become overwhelming. When you surrender to your destiny, it takes the pressure off you to keep up with the rest of society. Symptoms of this pressure include headaches, nausea, and breathing issues, so when you slow down and take your time, you will feel healthier and more grounded.

10) You Will Become Interested in Your Shared Synchronicities: Instead of being annoyed by the bonds that connect you, your shared interests and feelings will reassure you that, no matter what happens, this person will be in your life forever. You will become more aware that the things that are happening to you are probably happening to them as well. Send telepathic messages when you feel this connection and ask them to respond.

11) You Will Become More Interested in the Bond Between Science and Spirituality: Once you stop obsessing about what is going to happen in the future, you free up your mind to explore different subjects. If you were previously attracted to science subjects at school, you might seek knowledge from the spiritual world. Books about spirituality will appeal to you. Crystals and amulets will become part of your world while you feel the need to visit important spiritual places. Your next vacation may be somewhere as diverse as a retreat or a trip to India to visit a guru. If you are naturally spiritual, then the world of science will become appealing. Try subscribing to Science News, a bi-weekly publication that brings news from recent science and technical journals. The articles are short, professionally written, and packed with fascinating information written in layman's terms.

12) You Will be More Aware of the Changes in Your Twin's Tempo and How to Deal with Them: In the past, you may have felt these differences in mood and energy levels were a disruptive part of your relationship, but now you know better. You aren't meant to be completely in tune with each other because when you have different issues, you need to come together as a unit and deal with them. Even though you are separated, you still need to work in this way. Your telepathic connection doesn't mean they have constant access to your thoughts.

Here are simple ways you can improve your telepathic skills:

- **Start with Simple Messages and See How Clear They are When Your Partner Receives Them:** Send a color or shape to begin with, and then add another element.
- **Lose Fear:** Just like surrendering to the twin flame relationship, it's time to let go of negativity. Society may not believe in telepathy as a relevant way of communicating, but you already know it is. As twin flames, you have been communicating with each other for many lifetimes. Believe in your skill and accept that the more you practice, the better at it you will become.
- **Use Props to Improve the Strength of Your Signal:** Crystals, candles, and other aids help you concentrate and focus on your mission. Turn a room in your house into a spiritual place and use it to send your telepathic messages. You shouldn't limit your messages to your twin flame. Talk to the

universe and tell it your thoughts; it will listen and respond.

- **Power Up the Thought with Positivity:** When you send your thoughts, bathe them in a clear white light before you let them go. Feel the energy buzzing in your mind and send it to your chosen recipient.

- **Visualize Communication:** As you send your message, imagine how it will be received. Will your twin be joyful at your communication? Sometimes when you are apart, visualization will help you feel more connected.

There are codes and ethics connected to telepathy that shouldn't be ignored. Just as you value your privacy, so does your twin. Create a telepathic shield or cloak when you want to keep your thoughts secret. This should be something that both of you should do openly. You need to have mutual respect and be comfortable with your conversations on all planes.

13) You Will Experience Total Love: Once you let go of fear and doubt, you create the space for even more love. You recognize how your ego has distorted how you look at them, but now you have a clearer picture. This non-judgmental state of mind will let you recognize the depth of your love. They are amazing! They are the most amazing person in the universe. Your heart will swell with love and devotion for them even if you never meet them again.

14) When You Look into Their Eyes, You Will See a Representation of Your "Original" Environment: This is the origin of your soul. This is the place where you feel most comfortable. It can happen when you look into their eyes face to face, or it can happen even when separated. A picture of them may seem normal to other people, but it shines with energy to you. As you look into the eyes, you see a deep space lit with the divine light that fills your soul with hope. To you, your twin is like an angel in the darkness, always there to guide you and fill your soul with love.

15) You Will Feel a Purely Physical Pull: Once the spiritual connections are perfected, then the natural way to progress is on the physical plane. If the universe believes the time is right, it will put you on the right path to reconciliation. As with other situations, now is the time to follow the signs it sends you. If you suddenly receive an invitation to visit a new area, then accept it. If you see a deal on a trip that seems too good to be true, grab the opportunity, and it could lead you to your twin.

The universe is a minx when it comes to communicating with you! It can cause you to be affected by a sign simply designed to let you know it is there. A sense of physical touch could be a sign from the universe you are loved. If you feel a warm touch on your shoulder when you feel down, it is your divine self-giving you a positive sign. If you suddenly get goosebumps without the temperature changing, this means someone somewhere is having intense, passionate thoughts about you. A white feather or butterfly is also a classic sign you are communicating with the astral plane.

16) You Will Reach a Startling Conclusion About Your Relationship: You will both become accepting that your relationship with each other is the last and most complete union you will ever have. But what if this relationship doesn't survive your separation and fails to reach the reunion stage? That's okay as well. You have been part of the most intense and magical couplings imaginable.

Even if you are relatively young in human terms, your soul is not subject to the same aging process. If your soul is mature enough to accept that the relationship will survive no matter what the physical world throws at it, then it will be okay with the outcome. If your soul is relatively new to the spiritual realm, then it may experience some bruising. Don't worry; this is all part of your spiritual being's aging process, and you will emerge stronger and ready for your next union in another life.

17) You Will Discover a New Life Plan: Once you surrender to the process of twin flame unions, you will drop any false teachings that have governed your life previously. You will still be interested in environmental issues and feel an affinity to the planet, but you will know your place. Your life mission shouldn't be dedicated to healing any rifts in society or repairing any damage to the earth. Your mission should be about you, your love, and your connection with your twin. You are no longer interested in wasting time online envying other people. The world of celebrities and all the baggage they bring will be so irrelevant you wonder why it ever had any interest in the past. You will discover a thirst for knowledge that leads you to study more worthy subjects dear to your heart.

18) You Won't Care What Society Thinks Anymore: Your natural sense of style will emerge. You fail to conform and are more willing to flex your quirky personality. Your clothes may become more "out there," and you experiment more with your look.

19) You Will Embrace Your Inner Child: What did you love to do as a child? Do you still do it, or have you abandoned it as a childish pursuit. Maybe you loved to paint or draw as a child, but you don't have the time anymore. Make time. Instead of chilling out with Netflix, try hanging out with a sketchpad. Use your imagination to create works of art that reflect your personality. Surrendering is all about letting your natural instincts free.

Buy yourself skates or a skateboard and try out some moves at a local park. Who cares if you fall off and people laugh at you? You don't! Forget man-made teachings and how you appear to others. You have the perfect union with yourself when you form a connection with your flame, so all other opinions are muted. Did you ever regret something you didn't do? Then now is the time to do it. You have all the free time in the world once you let the universe take over your destiny, so use it to grow spiritually and physically.

20) You Will Relearn How to Experience Things: Next time you see a sporting event or an essential cultural experience on TV, consider what is happening. Are the people concentrated on what is happening, or can you just see a blanket of smartphones trying to picture the event? Modern society is so focused on recording events and experiences they have forgotten how to enjoy the natural joy and energy surrounding them. Leave your device at home and go out and experience the world. You don't care anymore what your online profile looks like, so why should you feel the need to photograph everything? Don't let technology interfere with your psyche. Let go of it and become a participant in life rather than a spectator.

When you surrender to your destiny, then you feel reborn. It is the highest form of acceptance and you recognize that any blocks you have in life are *your responsibility.* You will stop assigning blame to your twin, and when you do so, you will feel a purer form of love for them. When you make these personal shifts, you may find the obstacles that keep you apart from your twin disappear. The universe will determine if you are blessed with a reunion, and it will work tirelessly to get you together with them if that is your fate.

Chapter 10: Stage 7: Twin Flame Reunion or Joining

The end of the journey is in sight. The happily ever after a phase when you will both become one and the world will accept you as a couple. The separation will have been different for every couple. Your twin could have moved away and cut off all contact, or they may still live in the same house as you, but they have distanced themselves emotionally.

Maybe you and your partner have been stuck on the revolving wheel of separation and reunion for some time. You may have experienced exhausting cycles of drama and fear, followed by love and passion. This can happen when the two partners are at varying stages of spiritual growth. Unfortunately, some couples fail to reach the reunion stage as they are stuck in the 3D world and have failed to ascend. If this happens to you, don't worry; you have multiple lives ahead of you to reconnect with your twin flame.

The main thing to remember is this final union is unique for everyone and can follow varying periods of separation. Some people may have been apart for years as they both had issues that needed to be dealt with. Life is often complicated for twin flames as one or both halves of the couple may have emotional baggage that keeps them from committing.

Fortunately, some commonalities signal a reunion is about to happen. If you have experienced a feeling that your twin is using a "dangling carrot" type of thinking about your situation, then you may feel it's time to resolve your relationship. You will know when it is time to act and overcome your doubts and misgivings. This may cause a union between the two of you, or it may not. Whatever the outcome, when the signs occur, you must act on them. What happens next is determined by destiny and will give you peace of mind.

Signs That a Reunion is About to Happen

1) Excitement: Are you feeling butterflies in your stomach for no reason at all? Do you wake up with a feeling of joy and anticipation? This may be a sign from your heart chakra that something amazing is about to happen. Your soul is incredibly intuitive when it comes to your twin flame, and it will sense if a shift in their feelings has happened. You may have already surrendered to your union, but they may have held back. Internal excitement can signal they are now ready to reunite.

2) Communication Between the Two of You is More Harmonious: You may have had periods when all communications ceased or became fractious. You may have lost contact completely. If you suddenly find messages from them on social media or they appear in your dreams, then this is a sign they want to reconnect. Both of you may have moved since you last saw each other and are unaware of how to get in touch physically, but that won't stop you. Twin flames may be thousands of miles apart, but they will always be close on the astral plane.

3) Your Twin Flame Commitments May Have Changed: As a spiritual being, people in twin flame relationships have a common belief that their connection shouldn't interfere with another soul's contract on Earth. If your twin was already committed to someone else, then this may be part of the reason you separated. If you hear that their situation has changed, this may be a sign they will return to you. While this may be the perfect outcome for the two of you, be aware that other people will be hurt during the process. Spiritual wounds may be deeper than earthly ones, but the pain of separation is still considerable. But if you are currently putting your life on hold as you sit in a cosmic waiting room contemplating your twin and their partner breaking up, then you need to leave! Your twin has the free will needed to leave earthly relationships, and it is their choice to stay. You couldn't and shouldn't interfere. Get on with the rest of your life and find new opportunities for love.

4) The Reflection Principle: If thoughts of your twin have receded during your separation, you may be surprised to find yourself thinking about them a lot recently. This is a sign that something has shifted in your relationship, and you may be ready to reconcile. The term reflection principle means that if your thought patterns have changed, then so have your twins. Be aware that your counterpart feels the increase in intensity of feelings just as strongly as you do.

You may even find that their name crops up every time you converse with other people. If your friends and family have asked you how your twin is or if you have heard from them, take note! This is a sure sign from the universe they are destined to come back into your life. The spiritual plane is preparing you and your immediate circle of acquaintances for their reappearance. Watch out for old photos and memories that include your twin on social media. Facebook memories are especially attuned to your spiritual vibrations and can surprise you with a jolt from the past.

5) They Will Appear While You Meditate: If you have experienced signs that your twin is ready to reunite, but you aren't sure if this is true or merely wishful thinking, then try meditation for more concrete answers. This powerful tool is especially effective when you have questions that can't be answered by more traditional methods. Write down the purpose of your meditation on a piece of paper before you start the process. Now begin your chosen method of meditation and focus your thoughts on your twin flame. Ask if they are ready to become part of your union again. Are they going to be getting in touch soon, or are you misreading the signs? Sometimes you will feel like the answers you seek are beyond you, and even meditation is proving fruitless. Don't worry; the reasons you aren't getting answers may be beyond your control. There could be obstacles in place within yourself or your twin delaying the process. You are always given guidance, but you may have limiting barriers inside your psyche.

6) An Irresistible Draw to Places and Events: Do you feel like the universe is nudging you to get out more? This is a common sign that something is about to happen. We have discussed in other chapters how these signs may manifest. Sometimes you may be overwhelmed with conflicting signs hard to follow, or there may be a lack of input that makes you feel abandoned and alone. Take heart in the fact that the universe is a constant companion and is forever sending you information. When you are on a dark road and feeling like your future is uncertain, then you need only one light to guide you home. The dark road of your twin flame journey has been a rocky one, but the end is in sight.

The universe can lead you to a secondhand bookstore where you find a reference to a long-forgotten coffee shop you once used. When you revisit the coffee shop, you just happen to bump into a friend who knows your flame. You meet later in the week, and your twin reappears in your life.

You could even be involved in a minor car crash with a man who works with your twin flame. All coincidences will lead to your twin and a reunion. There are coincidences and blessings in disguise sent by the universe to nudge you in the right direction, so even the worst experiences can lead to positive outcomes.

7) Inner Peace: When you experience the surrendering phase, you automatically change your thought process. You understand that most things are out of your control, and that's okay. When you surrender, it is part of the process of awaiting reunion; however, paradoxically, when you give up on any chance of reunion, this can be the most potent sign of all. Once you find that all thoughts of a reunion and a happy life together have left you, you are in a state of inner wholeness. This radiates into outer wholeness, and when you realize that you need nobody else to complete you, or your life is the most likely time you will reunite.

8) You Feel Like They are with You Already: Have you felt like your twin is sitting right next to you? Has it reached the point where you turn toward them and starting a conversation even though you know they are miles away? When all barriers are down, and you are both spiritually ready for a reunion, then you will experience it on an astral plane first. Your divine timings are attuned, and the universe is preparing you both. You may even feel the need to adjust your home to be ready for your union. You will know instinctively if they are coming to you or if you need to move. You may find yourself looking at real estate in certain areas or checking out job vacancies in other areas. You will feel the spirit of your twin sharing their thoughts with you when you least expect it, and you will be comforted by their spiritual presence.

9) You Will Become More Creative: If you find yourself contemplating writing a novel for the first time or find yourself reading poetry, then a recoupling with your twin may be in the cards. Your soul may typically be more interested in practicalities and keeping your life ordered and organized, but you also feel energized as you feel more excited. Your creative juices will start flowing as you become more entwined with nature and beauty. You know the world is an amazing place to be, and you will feel an overwhelming desire to capture its beauty artistically. These pieces of creativity will give you something to share with your twin as you reunite. You are about to enter your union's highest expression, and you want to surround yourself with positive images and literature.

10) Recognize How Numbers Can be Used to Send Messages: Spiritual messages can take various forms, but one of the most powerful can be numbers. This could be because, during a regular day, we are inundated with numerical influences.

Consider these examples:

- When you pay a bill online, what do you need? A customer number, a card number, a final sum of how much to pay, and maybe a time of delivery are all necessary. These aspects are numerical.

- When traveling, what is the most important thing you need to check? Time, of course. What time is your train leaving, how long will the journey take, and what time is your connection?

- Shopping: Everything you buy has a monetary value. Every receipt will contain a multitude of numbers.
- Going to the Gym: If you think you can avoid numbers when getting fit, think again! You will have a certain number of reps to do and different exercises are designed to last for a specific length of time.
- Chill Out: Even at our most relaxed time is an important part of our routine. What time is your favorite program on? How many hours can you spend playing Xbox?

With this in mind, is it any wonder that the universe uses the power of numbers to influence us and remind us they are in control. Understanding what the numbers mean is an art that needs to be learned.

How to Recognize What Numbers are Trying to Tell You

Some people call the spiritual use of numbers numerology, while others call the process angel numbers. The reasoning behind sequences and their meanings are based on the geometric plan of the universe. While the spiritual guides that govern your life are constantly communicating with you, they know that the spiritual journey you are on is particularly important. Your twin will be receiving similar levels of guidance and will also be subject to numerical influences.

Master Numbers

The first of the master numbers is 11, the second is 22, and the third is 33. They represent the intuition and insight connected to your subconscious and gut feelings. Within the twin flame experience, they can play a major part in influencing you to ready yourself for a meeting or reunion between the two of you. Chances are, you will have witnessed the appearance of the first master number, 11, as you entered the yearning phase. Still, as you prepare yourself for a reunion, you will find it playing a special role in your life once again.

The perfect angel number is 1111, and it acts as a spiritual wake-up call to get ready for momentous events. So, if you are shopping in a store and your receipt is a sequence of 1's, then this tells you that you are currently part of the energy of the earth. Your cleansed spirit is at the perfect point to reach the zenith of your relationship. If the sequence is interspersed with the number 5, this can also be significant and indicate that positive times lie ahead. The number 8 signifies that a positive opportunity is in the cards for you.

Platonic relationships between twin flames can also gain guidance from numerology. The master number 11 can be combined with the number 7 to indicate a strong union that isn't based on sex or attraction. The sequence 7117 or 717 can be causally related to the tarot card that depicts the Lover. But, as tarot readers will tell you, this doesn't necessarily mean a sexual union. The numbers 6 and 9 will also make an appearance if you need a nudge to change your focus. 6 is an indication that you may be focusing too much on negative aspects, while 9 suggested that you are too focused on the material parts of your life. Both numbers indicate you should return to more spiritual pursuits.

The master number 22 is sent by your guides to encourage you to be more confident. Often referred to as the *master-builder*, it is used to encourage you to turn dreams into reality. It is meant to fill you with hope for the future and a confident outlook for your relationship.

With your relationship's reunion stage, you will be sent connections containing the master number 33. It is often called the master teacher and is more powerful because it is a combination of 11 and 22, which elevates it to the top level. The number 33 has no personal message to send. Instead, it is a sign that all humanity is about to experience a higher level of emotion. For those people waiting for signs of a possible reunion, it is a sign you have achieved a higher spiritual plane. Signs of the number 33 combined with recurring 11's are the most significant signs from your guide that your reunion is imminent.

What Happens Once You Have Rejoined Your Twin?

Once the separation phase has ended and you have both surrendered to your union, then the reunion will happen. You can't force it or screw it up; it just happens when you are both ready for this connection. You know you are meant to be together, and your subconscious minds will begin to merge, and you will be aware of each other's individual explicit awareness.

You Understand Three Things

1) The Significance of Your Partnership: You know each other so well that you are comfortable with your separate roles within the relationship. You may be a typical male/female couple who believe that your sex governs your roles. The woman will become responsible for the relationship's mental health and will take charge of the communication between you. The male partner will take on the role of protector and be responsible for the home and feeding the family. Less conventional couples will feel comfortable enough to assign roles without gender influences. The important thing to remember is that you are comfortable with your relationship and you can be honest with one another.

2) When You Work Together, You Form an Unbeatable Team: In the past, you will have had conflicts with the power you have in the union. You separated for a reason, and one of the main reasons could be you resisted working together. Now you have reunited, you are confident in your individual strengths, and you know that you are peerless when you combine your efforts.

3) You are Meant to Live Together: In the past, you may have struggled to live under the same roof because you need your personal space. Now you could live in a cupboard and be happy! You have recognized that being together anywhere makes that place the best place in the world. You will no longer argue over where you will live; you will decide together.

Conclusion

Are you ready to meet your twin flame? Does the thought of such an intense experience appeal to you, or are you still hesitant? This book was written to help you regardless of the stage you are in. Hopefully, it has helped you realize who is in your life for a specific reason and who will be there for you, always. Life is all about the relationships you form. Good luck in making the right choices, and remember, keep looking for signs from the universe!

Here's another book by Mari Silva that you might like

Your Free Gift (only available for a limited time)

Thanks for getting this book! If you want to learn more about various spirituality topics, then join Mari Silva's community and get a free guided meditation MP3 for awakening your third eye. This guided meditation mp3 is designed to open and strengthen ones third eye so you can experience a higher state of consciousness. Simply visit the link below the image to get started.

https://spiritualityspot.com/meditation

References

A Little Spark of Joy - Everything Tarot and life's Higher Vibes. (n.d.). Retrieved from https://www.alittlesparkofjoy.com/

ASK ANGELS For Help With Any Request! Contact Your Angels. (n.d.). Askingangels.com.

containhe01. (n.d.). Containhe01. Retrieved from https://www.newagedream.com/

CosmicMinds.com is for sale. (n.d.). HugeDomains. Retrieved from https://www.hugedomains.com/domain_profile.cfm?d=cosmicminds&e=com

Elite Daily. (n.d.). Elite Daily. https://www.elitedaily.com/

Forever Conscious. (n.d.). Forever Conscious. https://foreverconscious.com/

Hack Spirit. (n.d.). Hack Spirit. Retrieved from https://hackspirit.com/

Home. (n.d.). HipLatina. Retrieved from https://hiplatina.com/

Home - Awake and Align | Beyond Quantum Healing Hypnosis. (n.d.). Awake and Align. Retrieved from https://awakeandalign.com/

My Twin Soul Journal. (n.d.). My Twin Soul Journal. Retrieved from https://mytwinsouljournal.blog/

Nast, C. (n.d.). Allure - Beauty Tips, Trends & Product Reviews. Allure. Retrieved from http://www.allure.com

PowerofPositivity. (n.d.). Power of Positivity: #1 Positive Thinking & Self Help Community. Power of Positivity: Positive Thinking & Attitude. Retrieved from https://www.powerofpositivity.com/

Simply the best online psychic readings available anywhere - Psychic Elements. (n.d.). Psychicelements.com. Retrieved from https://psychicelements.com/

Supernatural Vibrations Home. (n.d.). Supernatural Vibrations. Retrieved from https://www.supernaturalvibrations.com/

The Mother Loving Future- Consciousness + Parenting. (n.d.). The Mother Loving Future. Retrieved from http://www.themotherlovingfuture.com/

Torgerson, R. (2019). Cosmopolitan.com - The Women's Magazine for Fashion, Sex Advice, Dating Tips, and Celebrity News. Cosmopolitan; Cosmopolitan. http://www.cosmopolitan.com

Twin Flamez – Zero's & One's with some added Two's. (n.d.). Retrieved from https://www.twinflamez.com/

Walk the path less traveled ⋆ LonerWolf. (n.d.). LonerWolf. Retrieved from http://www.lonerwolf.com

(2021). Orchidrecovery.com.

Germain, M. J. (2019). Opening the Akashic Records: Meet Your Record Keepers and Discover Your Soul's Purpose. Bear & Company.

Howe, L. (2009). How to Read the Akashic Records: Accessing the Archive of the Soul and Its Journey. Sounds True.

Howe, L. (2015). Discover Your Soul's Path Through the Akashic Records. Hay House Inc.

Ortiz, E. (2014). The Akashic Records: Sacred Exploration of Your Soul's Journey Within the Wisdom of the Collective Consciousness. Weiser.

https://www.youtube.com/watch?v=Bvo9YngPrpQ

https://www.divinebalance.eu/wp-content/uploads/2013/12/The-Value-of-an-Akashic-Records-Reading.pdf
https://www.manmeetkumar.com/post/7-awesome-ways-akashic-records-can-transform-your-life
https://intothelight.news/files/2020-03-03-akashic-records.php
https://darkascent.org/blog/2017/02/04/what-are-the-akashic-records-and-how-can-you-learn-to-access-them/
https://missmuslim.nyc/alchemy-astrology-akashic-records-islam/
https://en.wikipedia.org/wiki/Book_of_Life
https://books.google.com.eg/books?id=WvRiDwAAQBAJ&pg=PT26&lpg=PT26&dq=alice+bailey+akashic+records&source=bl&ots=qKDrA0Qdff&sig=ACfU3U2L-s3dEIKZIJuaFWM-RFA5bZS6vQ&hl=en&sa=X&ved=2ahUKEwjh782ZxbbpAhVSz4UKHaHvDo44ChDoATAAegQIBxAB#v=onepage&q=alice%20bailey%20akashic%20records&f=false
https://www.cherylmarlene.com/dispelling-myths-and-erroneous-notions-about-the-akashic-records/
https://medium.com/holisticism/what-are-the-akashic-records-ede3bee05673
Howe, L. (2009). How to Read the Akashic Records: Accessing the Archive of the Soul and Its Journey. Sounds True.
Taylor, S. A. (2018). The Akashic Records Made Easy: Unlock the Infinite Power, Wisdom, and Energy of the Universe. Hay House UK.
https://en.wikipedia.org/wiki/Theosophy#Personal_development_and_reincarnation
https://www.edgarcayce.org/the-readings/akashic-records/
https://michellebeltran.com/exploring-past-lives-akashic-records/
https://www.soulmastery.net/connect/akashic-record-past-life-readings/
https://medium.com/holisticism/what-are-the-akashic-records-ede3bee05673
https://drlesleyphillips.com/past-lives/past-life-regression/

https://www.amazon.com/Radical-Approach-Akashic-Records-Vibration-ebook/dp/B07G681W74
https://www.healyourlife.com/how-to-find-your-purpose-in-the-akashic-records
https://www.akashicrecordsinstitute.com/unlocking-the-hidden-healing-aspect-of-the-akashic-records/
https://www.soulandspiritmagazine.com/10-ways-the-akashic-records-can-heal-your-life/
Howe, L. (2009). How to Read the Akashic Records: Accessing the Archive of the Soul and Its Journey. Sounds True.
https://akashicknowing.com/wp-content/uploads/25-Akashic-Healing-Prayers-To-Transform-Your-Life-ebook.pdf

Made in United States
Troutdale, OR
12/21/2024

27167515R00126